M000281206

A YOUTH WRITING
BETWEEN THE WALLS

Notebooks from the Lodz Ghetto

Avraham Cytryn

Yad Vashem Jerusalem 2005

A YOUTH WRITING BETWEEN THE WALLS
Notebooks from the Lodz Ghetto

Avraham Cytryn

Translated from the Hebrew by Chaya Naor
Edited by Su Newman

© 2005 Yad Vashem
P.O.B. 3477, Jerusalem 91034
Email: publications.marketing@yadvashem.org.il

ISBN 0-9764425-1-5

Typesetting: Gary Rimmer
Production: Docostory Ltd., Raanana, Israel
www.docostory.com

CONTENTS

SCENES FROM THE GHETTO

AVRAHAM CYTRYN POET

MEMORIES

Introduction

Lodz 1940 – Paris 1994: A diptych

When, for the first time, you hold Avraham Cytryn's notebooks in your hand – notebooks filled with illegible passages, direct traces of the destruction taking place so close by – you cannot help but feel that you have come across a precious discovery. The white patches that occasionally break up the descriptions return the reader to the source of these stories, written in the Lodz ghetto by a young boy.

Avraham Cytryn was born in Lodz on October 10, 1927. When he was 13, a pupil in the Katznelson secondary school, his family was interned in the ghetto.

We are all familiar with the amazing precision of the children's drawings in the Terezin camp, a precision that gives them the documentary value of a chronicle. In these notebooks, in contrast, under the heavy burden of the events, the childish handwriting is actually charged with horrible maturity. It has the power to revive the sights – pictures from the life of the ghetto, living people, in their suffering or grotesqueness. Because Avraham Cytryn never stopped smiling even when faced with the things he was living and seeing, and sometimes, when he is unable to rely on humor, he speaks in poetry, but he regrets this lack no less than the lack of bread.

> The spark of humor has been extinguished in me
> I, who so wanted to burst into laughter
> How to go on living like this
> Without humor, like beasts?

The text of the stories has been deprived of the pause in time that every narrative takes when relating to the events described in it. But these stories resemble dreams intertwined as one whole with the events of the previous night. This is the special time of the world of concentration camps, dominated by two opposite trends: the slowness of movement and gaze, resulting from fatigue, and the constantly occurring vicissitudes that make life-or-death determinations with intractable speed. In this text, there is a fuzzy light attached to the words, or perhaps it is actually the absence of light, an unceasing blend of reality and imagination, a rough script like that in pre-historic paintings. In 1942, Yaacov, Avraham's father, died of hunger and exhaustion. At the end of August 1944, Avraham left his (unfinished) notebooks behind; the family was deported to Auschwitz, and Avraham never returned. His sister, Lucy, four years older than he, survived. She knows exactly how Avraham died: three days after he came to the camp and was separated from his mother and sister, he joined a group of children who had been promised an extra portion of soup. He was gassed with the entire group.

Lucy remembers that her brother, while he was still in the ghetto, was gripped by his obsession to write, and was engrossed in his notebooks every spare hour he had left after his work in the knitting workshop. He was consumed by the same subjects and repeated the same images again and again in his poetry and in his prose. The unfinished story, "Aliza or Forbidden Love," which tells of the forbidden love between a Jew and a German woman, ends with a poem entitled "Love through the Barbed Wire," in which a beautiful blonde brings food to her lover interned in the ghetto. And the pathetic element lies not in the fact that the barbed wire separates them, but rather in the confession that the young Jew makes at the end: "Your kiss is a lovely gift...but I still would prefer your basket." This situation, in which the boy interned in the ghetto is consumed by the desire to begin a literary creation, which compels him to write, is obviously unique.

Manuscripts like this – with their textual layering, the lines climbing one upon the other and spilling over into the margins – seem to reveal the essence of writing in its most basic and primal role – rebellion against forgetting.

Avraham Cytryn not only sensed his impending death – not surprising in the conditions that prevailed in the ghetto – but he predicted it to the very day. It was as if the intuition of death, which was part of his entire creative output, became not only the source of his writing but in fact, its final destination. Moreover, beyond this intuition, every writer projects himself into the future, which extends him, if one can put it that way, and at the same time passes him by. The notebooks, therefore, are also engraved on the chain of generations originating in the Holocaust: today we know that the annihilation affected not only those directly harmed by it, but also their children and grandchildren. And this is what the notebooks tell us, beyond the bits of ghetto life that they present to us.

Avraham Cytryn wanted to commit suicide, but he did not do so, out of his compassion for his mother. The train took him to Auschwitz, together with his mother and sister. The notebooks remained in his home in the Lodz ghetto, except for one that Avraham took with him when he embarked on the journey to his death.

The first ghetto of Lodz existed from 1827-1861, when that part of Poland was under Russian rule. A decree issued by Czar Nicholas I required most of the Jews to live in one quarter, south of Podzena and Wolborska streets. Lodz was famous for its textile industry, and only Jews who owned factories were permitted to live outside the ghetto, but they were forbidden to wear their traditional clothing and their children went to Christian schools. In 1861, Czar Alexander II rescinded the order obligating the Jews to live in the delimited part of the city.

The second ghetto was established in 1940, in one of the poor neighborhoods of Baluty. 62,000 Jews were already living there, and another 100,000 lived in the city or the suburbs. It was the first operation of its kind carried out by the Germans, a dress rehearsal of sorts for the establishment of other ghettos in other places. The transfers, planned with great secrecy, were carried out with speed so that the Jews would be forced to abandon a large part of their belongings that would then be confiscated.

On February 8, 1940, the Poles and the "ethnic Germans" who lived near the ghetto were ordered to move away from there no later than February 29. On March 1, the Germans organized a pogrom, "bloody Thursday," and following it, thousands of Jews were herded into the ghetto. Given only a few minutes to prepare, they were expelled from their homes, neighborhood after neighborhood.

The first Jews arrived in the ghetto between February 12 and 17, and by April 30, all of the city's Jews had been transferred there. Lodz was given a German name, "Litzmannstadt," and the ghetto was called the "Litzmannstadt ghetto." It was the second largest ghetto, after the one in Warsaw.

When there were 164,000 Jews in the ghetto (70,000 others left the city), it was encircled by barbed wire fences and a wooden partition, and units of the *Schutzpolizei*, the municipal branch of the protection police, were stationed around it. On May 10, the *Polizeipräsident* of Lodz issued a regulation forbidding the Jews to leave the ghetto or Germans and Poles to enter it. Two passages crossed the ghetto and divided it into three parts, connected by three entrances for vehicles and three bridges for pedestrians, so the residents of the city could cross the ghetto in a tram and see some of its streets from the windows, without being permitted to really enter it. The isolation of the Jews was even more extreme because, as part of the "policy of Germanization," they were deliberately surrounded by a German population.

Inside this enclave, the Jews were forbidden to leave their dwellings between seven in the evening and seven in the morning. They continued to wear the yellow badge. The Gestapo opened an office inside the ghetto. The connections between the Jewish administrations and the ghetto administration, the *Ghettoverwaltung*, were handled by Hans Biebow in the Baluty market, where several German offices as well as the office of the Jewish Council were housed.

The Germans conceived the idea of establishing the Lodz ghetto as a very temporary means: its inhabitants were supposed to be transferred to "reservations" in the Lublin district or to Madagascar. But the Germans' plans changed, and in the end, this ghetto lasted longer than any of the others. It was maintained until 1944, and then the last of its residents left as they were taken to the extermination camps.

In September 1941, 8.5 persons per room crowded together in the ghetto's four square kilometers, making it simply impossible to maintain minimal sanitary conditions. At this stage, 144,000 people were living in the 25,000 rooms that were fit to be lived in. Although the area was very small, transport problems arose, and the municipal administration was forced to set up a new bus service traveling along the ghetto's boundary line.

Apparently, Lodz had the distinction of being the home of one of the most totalitarian bureaucracies, and the president of its "Council of Elders," Mordechai Chaim Rumkowski, became known as the "dictator of the ghetto." Rumkowski, a childless widower and small-scale industrialist, who had declared bankruptcy more than once, had devoted his time to charitable deeds before the war, and was in charge of the orphanage. When the ghetto was established, and positions were re-assigned, he chose (or was chosen) to be "king of the Jews," an office he filled highhandedly. He ordered that stamps be printed bearing his image, and then obtained German approval to print money. The ghetto workers were paid with these coins and bills. He was in the habit of traveling throughout the ghetto in a carriage, clad in a royal cloak. In his speeches, he would speak about "my children, my factories, my Jews." He was proud of the fact that he was keeping order and quiet in the ghetto. Not content to merely obey his German masters, he became intoxicated with his own power, and as befits any true tyrant, he demanded of his subjects not only their submission – which they would have given in any case – but their love as well. His court poets composed hymns in his honor and children wrote praises lauding "our beloved, wise president."

Rumkowski, who probably considered himself his people's savior, fell into a trap that turned him into a hangman. The lack of clarity as to the role of the Councils of Jews, which on the one hand, ensured the survival of Jews in the ghettos, and on the other, led to their destruction, was reflected in the administrative organization, which included divisions such as supply (food and coal warehouses, bread bakeries, 17 points of sale for milk, butter and other foodstuffs distributed according to medical instructions), welfare services (infant care centers, orphanages, old age homes, centers for the disabled, public canteens, children's institutions, etc.), public health (hospitals, clinics, dental clinics, pharmacies, disinfection service), but also a police force comprising six hundred policemen armed with clubs, who emulated the German model in every way and intervened everywhere when offenses against the regulations could have eased the harsh conditions of the ghetto's residents. When protest demonstrations began, inspired by underground rebels – Bundists, Zionists and Communists – Rumkowski punished them severely and persecuted these resistance movements as if they had committed the crime of showing contempt for his majesty's honor. The survival of the ghetto, which had been completely cut off from the outside world, depended on purchases that only the Judenrat could make. Foodstuffs bought on the black market or obtained from smugglers and the vegetables grown locally were far from enough. Even from this scant supply, the Germans took as big a slice as possible, and exported products to Germany that were meant for the ghetto. As a result, the ghetto received only minute quantities of food, and of the worst kind. The food regimen of the ghetto inhabitants soon became that of a German prison, and from 1941 was reduced even further. The administration of the Litzmannstadt ghetto – which was dependent on the Judenrat – undertook to manage all its affairs.

While it was the Germans who decided on the general quantities of food sent to the ghettos, it was the Judenrat that distributed it in the area. From the very beginning, a state of inequality reigned. The workers in the canteens were the first to eat, and they stole food to sell. Some of the ghetto inhabitants were impoverished while others had managed to keep some objects, which made it easier for them to purchase food and other necessities. Food shops called "cooperatives" operated in the ghetto, but a part of the groceries disappeared into the black market. The canteens, and later the cooperatives that belonged to political parties recognized by Rumkowski – the Bund and certain Zionist parties – were "nationalized." But this change made no difference at all. In the end, the Judenrat gave additional ration coupons to certain groups in the population: forced laborers, doctors, and pharmacists. It announced these additions each week in notices affixed to the store windows. The office holders were the main ben-eficiaries. All the others knew exactly what they had been deprived of for the good of others.

The policemen ate the food packages provided for the ghetto; as for the packages that came by mail, Rumkowski banned anyone from using them, so that the population depended entirely on the rations that he distributed.

The ghetto population, starved and systematically robbed by the Germans who continued to confiscate anything they could still find among the Jews, such as furs, bed linen, or musical instruments, dwindled month after month. The epidemics had a disastrous effect: typhus in the summer, tuberculosis in the fall, and influenza in the winter. The crowded conditions were ideal for the spread of fleas, and malnutrition contributed its share in weakening the body. More and more corpses lay in the streets, until the death wagon could come and collect them.

When the ghetto was established, the Germans expected it to supply enough work to meet its own needs. In actual fact, because the ghetto was isolated, its economic ties with the outside world were soon severed. The last Jewish factories still in existence were transferred to Aryan ownership. The population had no work, and most of the Jews interned in the ghetto had no means of livelihood. The situation improved a little when a network of factories began producing items of equipment for the Wehrmacht. In August 1942, 91 factories in the ghetto employed 77,982 workers. Many of them, however, did not earn enough to pay for the miserable rations allotted to them, and their working conditions were unbearable. Moreover, the population had good reasons to fear the hunts intended to supply workers for the labor camp in Warthegau. From 1940-1944, 15,000 Jews were sent to labor camps; very few returned, and those who did were in a state of total collapse.

From May 1940 to September 1942, the Germans allowed a relative degree of autonomy in the ghetto, but after a wave of mass deportations to the Chelmno extermination camp, they changed their policy. From January to April 1942, 44,000 Jews were taken to the camps. In May 1942, 11,000 Jews from Prague, Vienna, Luxembourg and other regions of Western Europe, were deported to camps. Afterwards, 16,000 Jews from Lodz were taken to camps, including children less than ten years old, and the elderly or weak. On October 1, 1942, there were only 89,446 persons left in the ghetto, even with the addition of 15,000 Jews from other ghettos, which had been annihilated.

After these extermination operations, the Germans turned the ghetto into a labor camp. They reduced the number of offices in the Jewish administration that had been in charge of the population's needs – health, education, religion, etc. They also closed the orphanages, old people's homes and most of the hospitals and schools. In August 1943, the number of factories increased to 119. Now 90 per cent of the population was employed in them. Children, eight years or older, also worked. Rumkowski's authority was restricted. The ghetto went on in this way until it was finally liquidated between June and August 1944. In September 1944, the entire population left in the ghetto – 76,701 men, women and children – was sent to Auschwitz.

The story is told that during the deportation, Rumkowski asked for a special car for himself and his family, to be attached to the rear of the train, so that he could travel to Auschwitz in conditions befitting his status...

In January 1945, only 800 Jews were left in the ghetto, members of the *Aufräumungs-kommando*, who were assigned the task of destroying the ghetto. There were also some individual Jews who hid there. The Soviet army liberated them on January 19, 1945.

After she was liberated, Lucy Cytryn returned to Lodz. There she found her brother's notebooks, where he had left them, in the family's apartment in the ghetto. In them, she discovered several stories and hundreds of poems.

In 1950, when Lucy and her husband left Lodz on their way to Israel (which they later left to live in France), the Polish customs official cut open the suitcase that contained the manuscript, and all the pages were scattered on the floor. Some were lost, creating more blank spaces in these documents that had been saved from deportation and annihilation.

A year after Auschwitz, Lucy's hair grew back in again, and before very long she married. Her name changed to Lucy Bialer and she gave birth to a daughter, Nellie. Lucy couldn't bear to look at Nellie's smooth head that reminded her of only one thing: the camp. She insisted on putting hats on her baby daughter's head, but Nellie kept pulling them off angrily.

And here the struggle against forgetting begins, a struggle that each of the survivors waged in their own way. Lucy and her husband, who was a survivor of Treblinka (and had spent time in other camps as well), transmitted information verbally. It was their daughter Nellie who heard and stored their experiences. She was also the one to whom Lucy entrusted Avraham's notebooks in the hope that she would publish them some day. But she did not, fearful of reawakening the painful past and wishing to spare her parents a return to the inferno. So Nellie maintained the heavy burden of silence, living with the memory of a past that was not her past, until the end: when she was forty she succumbed to the cancer that had spread through her brain.

After Nellie's death, Lucy Bialer decided to live, for the sake of the memory of her daughter and her brother. To live and to write. Nearly fifty years had passed from the time her brother had described the events until his sister decided she would answer him from the other side – from this future he had envisaged at the time in its tersest and bloodiest form. In doing so, she completed a pageant of many fragmented voices, which, although they could not describe the reality of the Holocaust – clearly an impossible task – could at least evoke in us a tremor no less intense.

Avraham's notebooks are so intense that an intermediary is needed to transmit them to the reader, and only someone who has undergone the same experiences can serve as such a go-between. Lucy Bialer's testimony creates the connection between the events her brother described in fictional form and the life of the family depicted today in her memoirs. Thus, a painting opens for the reader on two panels, a diptych conducting a dialogue that continues to resonate over a gap of half a century: the two voices provide an echo that connects the years that have passed and the silence that stretches between them, an echo that until now had lain dormant in the tunnel of time.

The rebellion that Avraham Cytryn expresses in his writing is not only a cry that imminent death and the debasing conditions of life wrenched from his heart. Avraham is settling accounts with all the authorities and powers that threatened his writing, including the family. In the Waronsky family, for example, the protagonist sees his father burning his poems. This episode was inspired by real life: Avraham, who from an early age, had resolved he would not follow the path laid down by his family, which had established one of the first textile finishing factories in the city, had experienced this humiliation himself and decided to become a poet. Of course, he also makes disparaging comments about the master of the ghetto, Rumkowski, mocking his pretentious notion of himself as an exalted figure. He describes the secret, unprecedented relations that take shape in the world of the concentration camps, the new hierarchy, which is structured by only one force – the place of each and every person awaiting death in the queue.

Somewhere between the stories of the brother and sister, in this fifty-year long silence, one finds the reason for testifying to the inferno: it is imperative to transmit it to the coming generations, for without it no life is possible. It allays the fervent desire for suicide, and when death does come and severs the chain of the generations, writing acquires its *raison d'être*. At this stage, the piece of writing is more than a recounting of what happened; it also gives form to the description, a form that restores to life what has been taken from it. And this may be the point that is made in the letter written by Robert Antelme to Dionys Mascolo in 1945:

"On this matter, I should like to say other things to you that I think are important, but I understand that in doing so I will be taking a very serious risk: D, I think I no longer know what one says or does not say. In hell one says everything, and by the way, I assume that is precisely the hallmark that enables us to identify it."

The survivors' first task was to talk. The very next task, oddly enough, was to refrain from telling everything, to organize what they were saying so that the hell they experienced would be comprehensible to others.

What to tell and what not to tell? Lucy Cytryn-Bialer asks herself. So many things have already been said that it is impossible to hear them again. Other things could not be uttered, precisely because they are unlike anything else in human experience. The past that is engraved on the present is what cannot be translated, except by two voices, because only a double echo can make this wound heard. A wound that affects not only one person, one population, one generation, but tears the very fabric of all time.

Luba Yurgenson

STORIES

A Mother's Terrible Crime
A True Story from the Litzmannstadt Ghetto

The Beigelman Family

At the corner of Pieprzowa Street, on the third floor of an apartment house entered through a narrow wooden staircase, live Shura Beigelman, her small son Eli and her sickly daughter Benitza. The family lives in awful filth. "How can you keep a proper home in this accursed ghetto?" Shura cried out. "Only the 'big shots' can afford such luxuries!"

Shura, a simple, poor woman from Pieprzowa, does not belong to the privileged class. If you have any doubts, all you need to do is look at the ceiling lined with cracks through which muddy rain constantly drips. Even before you enter the house, you're assailed by the stench of excrement and other muck. Wrinkled clothes lie in a pile on the floor, and smelly, stained sheets are heaped on broken pieces of chairs carelessly scattered around the room. Your eyes take in an awful sight, dominated by poverty, darkness and resignation, the result of the dreariness of days without end.

Shura's prematurely old face and her half-mad gaze give her the look of a modern witch scrambling among the heaps of dirty bed linen and the full chamber pots. The ceramic stove standing in the center of the room gives off heavy black clouds, like a smokestack. The autumn, especially cruel to these people, already burdened by inhuman suffering, drops its useless tears on the bed where Shura's two children are sleeping...

Blackened by soot, Shura blows with satanic persistence

on the bricks of extinguished coal lying, nearly cold, on the grid of the stove. It no longer gives off heat, only dark columns of smoke rising towards the ceiling, and then spreading throughout the room. It's hard for Benitza to bear the smoke, and she reacts with horrible bursts of coughing, that do not give her a moment's respite. The poisoned air is destroying her body. She coughs in a dark corner, shaking her small, thin arms with heartrending movements, her whole body trembling. The spasms contort her tiny face.

How badly the child reacts to these attacks that torment her poor body! How brutally fate plagues her! The small child has never known any other life but this – so monotonous, sickly, as bitter as wormwood. But nonetheless, she has grown accustomed to the smoke, her great enemy, and regards it as an inevitable guest.

When the cloud of smoke dispels slowly, Benitza's breath becomes more regular, the attack passes, and a pale, innocent smile flowers again upon her bloodless lips. Her clear blue eyes gaze upon the room. They glitter and seem to be saying: "I too have a right to live, the embers of life glow in me too."

Shura stops breathing, once again trapped in an awful fit of coughing. She spits on the rotting floor. Passionate curses flow from her thick lips: "*A schwarz tzibrochene geta leiben!*"[1]

Concealed under the warm blanket, Eli suddenly awakens. A small, bald head peers carefully from the bed, and a pair of panicky eyes survey the smoke-filled room. The child sits up on the bed, motionless, attempting to see

---

[1] Yiddish: "The black, broken life of the ghetto."

through the thick screen of smoke. Drip, drop, a raindrop falls on his head.

"Mama," the boy calls out, "it's raining in the house!"

"What do you want me to do, my little one…I've sealed up all the holes in the ceiling with rags, but it does no good. The cruel wetness seeps in through the material, and the water continues to flow. Yesterday I ran to the housing office, where I had to wait for hours until I could submit my complaint. The clerk reminded me again and again that he was very busy, and that I had to make it short. I had tears in my eyes and began speaking in Polish, but I was stammering so much that everything got mixed up in my head. Then I began the story all over again in Yiddish. The clerk didn't understand anything, and grew angry. Finally, he grabbed his bowl and quickly got into the soup line. I waited patiently for at least half an hour. Everyone made it clear to me that I shouldn't stay in the office. Grand ladies and gentlemen – the kind who have connections – they all came in and arranged their affairs in a minute. Nearly all the men were wearing boots, they looked so arrogant. And I, huddled there in my corner, so very small. All the time, they looked at my terrible clothes and my tattered slippers. They looked at my old face with contempt. We are really all alone in the world. Oh, my son, what a disaster, this ghetto! And for us it's even worse than for others! And when I think that before the war I had a grocery store, with vegetables and chocolates and cheeses…just the thought of it makes my mouth water."

Shura draws closer to the two pictures hanging above the bed. One is of her, the other of her husband, Zuzik Beigelman. Healthy faces, full of color and the joy of life. And she begins to mutter curses and vulgarities in Yiddish.

Eli sticks his little bald head out of the bed, his large eyes dark and frightened.

"Momma! Momma! I'm wet! I can't sleep! And tomorrow I'm working, don't forget!"

The room is dark with smoke. It's impossible to breathe the air. "Maybe it won't be so wet if I add some wood," Shura thinks. "This miserable fire is warming us up a bit despite everything."

Benitza sits on the floor near the window, trying to find a little clean air. Shura, bending over the stove, blows and blows, and her face becomes covered with soot. "Stay here a little longer," she says to her daughter. "I'll try to get the fire going." "I can't bear seeing Momma like this, so sad and exhausted all the time," Benitza thinks. But the child can't express her thoughts because she's mute. That's why she looks at the horrible, cruel world in silence. That's what the good Lord wanted, but she understands everything. To communicate with Eli, she uses her hands and eyes.

Shura only rarely kisses her daughter, but she tries to envelop her with tenderness. Benitza for her part loves her little mother very much, even though she can never tell her in words how much she loves her. When her asthma gives her a bit of rest, she affectionately caresses her mother's wrinkled face and her eyes fill with sadness. Then she resembles a blossoming flower. The worst hours are those when Shura and Eli are at work, and she remains alone in this small, wretched room. When she is alone, she can't stop crying, her eyes fastened on the door, waiting for her beloved mother and brother to return.

Eli sleeps alongside Benitza, and his mother and sister's coughing constantly wake him up. He sits up for a minute, an alarmed look on his face, and finally gets up: "Let's get up - go to work, go to work!" Large drops fall on his head. "Mother, the cracks in the ceiling are getting bigger! We need to put an umbrella up there!" he shouts. Children always think that their mother can do anything, that's the way of the world! Shura weeps, her arms lifted upward towards the heavens.

A Day in the Litzmannstadt Ghetto

"What a hellish life!" Shura thinks, as she tries to drive away the bad memories that assault her. As if she were at the cinema, she sees ghostly pictures passing before her. The yellow face of Zuzik, her consumptive husband, appears in front of her eyes, his awful groans piercing her ears. Then she sees again how they were expelled from their apartment and moved to the ghetto: the desolate city, the moans and sobs of the victims crowding into the enclosure, the black hearse, the body wrapped in a beautiful white shroud...death! Brrr! Shura shudders, and then, breathing hard, she again bends over the black stove. Her constricted chest rises and falls, like a sledgehammer. "Finally, the fire has caught," she calls in relief, and places a tin containing the leftovers of yesterday's coffee on the grid. She quickly walks to the corner where a few yellow turnips are lying. She selects one, quite fat, slightly distorted in shape, and begins peeling it. She attacks the vegetable, which is actually food for farm animals, and throws the tough peels into a pail. Her aquiline nose drips snot. She wipes it away with a practiced movement of her hand. That's what poverty which knows no aesthetics has taught her!

Eli, it's seven thirty, time to go to work, she yells to her son. The child's silhouette, motionless until then, comes to life. He rubs his eyes. Outside the rough voices of the men removing the excrement ring out. Wearing a white shirt, the boy slowly gets out of bed. His teeth are chattering, as if he were feverish. "*Kalt!*"[2] he groans, and dresses quickly. He washes his small purple face and blue hands. Then he

---

[2] Yiddish: cold.

29

goes over to the closet, opens it, removes three hundred grams of bread, and examines it from all sides. With a knife, he cuts off a slice for himself, and breathes in the delectable smell with pleasure. "Momma, Give me a little oil!" the starving boy calls to his soot-covered mother. "Can't you eat dry bread?" Shura replies in a bad temper. "Take a radish, you rascal! The oil is for frying food! If I give it to you, we won't last until we get the next rations!" "I want oil!" the hungry boy cries, stamping his feet like a small animal. "All right, then, I'll give you oil, you greedy boy! If you eat all three hundreds grams of your bread today, tomorrow you'll die of hunger!"

Eli puts on an old, ragged coat, goes quickly down the old wooden stairs and blends into the crowd of people going to work.

The cruel ghetto has left its imprint on the black pupils of his eyes, which look like blood clots in a deep wound. In his gaze there is a mystical expression that his life of suffering and the monotony of the days, devoid of any joy, have made even gloomier. A purplish face, pale skin tinged with yellow, black, worried, dulled eyes that light up only at the sight of soup – all the signs that this boy with his shaven head is a child of the Litzmannstadt Ghetto. He is thin, weak, skeletal, nervous. And even so, he is not part of the army of the living dead of the ghetto. He still walks normally, and his small face, more or less human, is still pleasant.

And just then, out of the fog, a blue-green face of one of those walking corpses appears. His head is stuck stubbornly on haggard shoulders, his teeth rigid with hunger and cold. His body nothing but a skeleton. The living dead advances slowly, like a turtle, his wide open eyes fastened to the ground, and on his way he spreads clouds of gloomy darkness. His movements are awkward, and he is as wizened as a newborn babe. From time to time, he fixes a suspicious look on the passersby. Fearful that they will push him, he slows his pace, and groaning, more precisely whining like a wretched, abandoned dog, he moves on with tiny steps. "Look," a woman wearing a kerchief whispers to her son, "A pale boy with thin, crooked legs!" – "Ah! A living-dead! Living-dead!" the child twitters, looking curiously at the strange creature from the world of truth. "A walking corpse!" an urchin yells, and then turns to him and mockingly says: "Hey, skeleton, you're eating our bread!"

It's seven o'clock; a regiment of exhausted workers gets up: the naked reality of the ghetto. It's eight o'clock; with drooping eyes, the *Arbeitsleute*[3] arrive in masses to their work, their yellow clogs angrily beating against the stones of the muddy street. Among them, walking quietly, at their own pace, are those with connections and all other types of shirkers, who now are doomed to be like everyone else, and they go to work as if they were going to the gallows. On the gray walls of the houses, the thin silhouette of the procession of skeletons is reflected as they make their way with mechanical steps towards their place of work, or in other words – to the slaughterhouse. In return for their labor, the foreman offers these workers soup the employees of the canteen, whom they all detest, apportion to them. But as far as they are concerned, it's a worthwhile transaction.

Eli lifts the collar of his threadbare coat because the rain

[3] German: the workers.

31

drips mercilessly into it. He looks like a marble statue sculpted by an artist to describe the epitome of humiliation. His typically Semitic look is likely to unleash the bloodthirsty rage of even the gentlest of Aryans. Eli does not have a long nose, nor are his movements nervous, but what eyes he has! Eyes that deserve to be immortalized...

The boy must have dallied on his way, because the bells have already struck eight, and throughout the ghetto, the racket of the machines, the sound of voices, the squeaking of saws, the ringing of the cars drawn by the Jewish tram, and the yells of the peddlers loudly hawking their candies are heard. *Die groise kletche! De groise bumbes!*[4] the peddlers yell out in their tireless voices, when little Eli, dizzy, stops near the coal shed to solve a difficult problem. The frightening squeal of a machine upsets the boy, and an idea that haunts him fills him with instinctive dread. Here, very close to him, one of the peddlers is loudly hawking his candies and cruelly arousing hunger in the poor stomachs of the passersby. "Candies made of cream and butter, sugar and milk! You've never seen anything like them! A remedy for the heart!" a giant shouts in a shrill bass voice. "Saccharine, saccharine!" a woman with a tinny voice sings out. "Vroom, vroom," the hellish machine near the coal warehouse rumbles. The policeman directing traffic waves his stick and curses the crowd. Move already, damn it! His yell affects startled Eli like the swish of a whip; at once he recovers his senses. The policeman's colorful peaked cap glows like a merry butterfly in the grayness of the crowd. An unsolved riddle keeps tormenting the wretched boy: his portion of bread, three hundred grams, lies in his left

4 Yiddish: "Large candies, large as bricks"

pocket, wrapped carefully. The boy begins to consider the situation logically: in my left pocket I have 300 grams of bread. Suppose I eat it all today, then I'll have to tighten my belt for two more days. Two days of fasting, I'll surely end up in the Marysin cemetery. Brrr! I'll still have some more time before I'm forced to sniff the wet ground in my grave. I'll leave 100 grams for tomorrow's breakfast, and the day after I'll fast.

Vroom, vroom, vroom, sure you'll drop dead, more than sure, it sounded as if the noisy machine was confirming the boy's thoughts.

At the Baluty market square,[5] Jewish millers, members of the "white guard," are loading sacks of flour, worth their weight in gold, on trucks. At the entrance to the market, there is always a hubbub. A German soldier pushes his way into his sentry post. A member of the Jewish guard service leans on the open door, a stick under his armpit. Opposite the Baluty market, at the entrance to the *Ordnungsdients*,[6] stands a young policeman in shiny boots, a pleasant smile on his lips. The hands of the ornate clock of the ghetto move slowly. But in Eli's eyes, their movement seems particularly tangible. "Eight ten, the pendulum mocks, you will not get there in time for sure, you snot-nosed kid." "Quick," a mysterious voice calls in his sensitive ear. The boy, aware of the danger threatening him, speedily makes his escape. As he runs, he fingers his left pocket, to make sure his treasure has not disappeared. A piece of bread has slipped a bit, but it is still there. Poor child! If he had lost it, he'd be desperate. Eli runs past a row of work-

---

[5] the location of the Jewish administration in the ghetto.
[6] The German guard service.

shops and offices. He lands on the first steps of the bridge, which rises up right in front of his nose, and then he is swallowed up in the commotion of the crowd.

At the top of the bridge, Eli is still beset by that same feeling: an illogical dread. Why is he so anxious? There's no danger that he'll fall because long gray walls would stop him. Underneath him, the trams move with a dull screech, from time to time igniting glowing sparks in the electric wires. German trucks, bearing the names of commercial companies, go by loudly. Cars and limousines speed past and vanish on the horizon, at the end of the narrowing street. To Eli, the trams look like fire-breathing dragons, and the cars like the daughters of Satan. The black swastikas make his blood run cold. In his thoughts, they are the symbol of a dire prediction. The world below breathes in evil, and the people in green uniforms are wicked, hostile and cruel like the Romans in Nero's time. They are distant, incomprehensible, alien. Seeing these barbarians, he feels an instinctive sense of dread. He will never forget their brutal, savage faces when they came to deprive the city's Jews of their homes and moved them to the ghetto. They are devils who escaped from hell on the day of judgment. He tries to look at them as little as possible, to avoid them whenever he can.

He walks off the bridge and goes towards Lutomierska St. He goes past the *Arbeitsamt*,[7] one of the better-known administrative offices of the ghetto, and turns into the alley where the carpentry shop is located. He hears the squealing of the saws, the banging of the machines and the shouts of the workers.

[7] German: The employment office.

Shamefacedly, he goes into the entryway. "Where do you think you're going?" the man at the gate asks him. "Ah...ah...to work," Eli stammers. "You come to work at eight-thirty? Go home at once! One more worker like you and it's the end of us! All right, just this once, go in, boy! One, two and..."

Before the man can count to ten, Eli passes through the entryway into the yard of the carpentry shop. "Ha, ha, ha," the man laughs wholeheartedly as he notices two workers resting on a bench. "Did you see that one? At his age he's already working! One more loyal servant of His Majesty Rumkowski! Ha, ha, ha!" The group in the entryway laughs loudly.

When Eli comes into the workshop, he encounters the severe, cold gaze of the foreman. Before the man can open his mouth, the red-faced boy is already muttering in a shaky voice, "there was a jam on the bridge, I couldn't pass, that's why I'm late..." "Liar!" the foreman yells, "There was no jam on the bridge today, you could have passed without any problem. Don't let it happen again, you little brat! And now, get to work!"

Eli obediently picks up his plane, and with his tongue hanging out, he begins to file down the loveliest beam in the pile. He devotes himself completely to his work. Everyone around him is working hard at full speed. The apprentices eagerly stand around the experienced foreman who is teaching them a new technique of carpentry. A cigarette hangs from the corner of his mouth, as he measures the polished beams handed to him by an apprentice wearing a work apron. The saw of the expert, Eliezer Rosen, squeals as he works, again and again wiping the sweat off his brow with his shirt-tail. The chips pile up, the workers are already wallowing in a layer of wood pulp. "Have you fellows heard about the new rations?" the amiable Eliezer asks. "It turns out it's going to be something really great," a boy wearing an apron continues. "Great for us, or for Beirat?"[8] Another apprentice asks amiably. The first man, offended, says: "Tell me, do you think I'm just throwing some words up into the air? If I told you where I got my information, you'd be amazed!" "So, go ahead, tell us everything," the foreman, his curiosity aroused, calls out. The workers all leave their stations and lend an ear. "It was Sheshzevslibi[9] in person who gave me this precious information…" "Well, are you going to tell us or not?" the foreman, breathing hard, interrupts him. "Dear sirs, each one will receive six hundred grams of sugar, seventy grams of flour…" All those present express their enthusiasm by excitedly clucking their tongues. "..four hundred grams of oatmeal.." "Ah!" the excitement mounts. "…three hundred grams of date starch…and what else…two hundred and fifty grams of jam, three hundred grams of a coffee mixture…" And Mr. Bluff gets carried away, as he describes this astounding ration. The eyes of his listeners glisten with wild joy. Bluff, alarmed at his own lies, is afraid to retreat now. I've gone too far, he thinks to himself. If I tell them the truth now, they'll kill me. At least, the rations I told them about have heated up the atmosphere. That's all they're talking about. In his mind's eye, Eli can already see himself sitting at the table, sipping black coffee, sugar and jam melting in his mouth. His mouth fills with saliva. The bread in his pocket begins to tempt him like the devil. I have to take a

---

[8] German: the Jewish leaders of the ghetto.
[9] The Minister of Supply in the ghetto. His name in Polish means "happy."

minute's break and eat a piece of it. No matter what! Eli takes out his bread ration and swallows it. "Didn't you eat breakfast?" the foreman asks him. Eli chokes, looking with wide open eyes at the boss. "Eat, eat," the man says, and goes back to indifferently measuring the beams.

For one brief moment, Eli is in paradise.

Of course, the rabbi that used to come to their home before the war, to give lessons in Judaism had told him about Adam and Eve. But for Eli, the temptation of the bread seems much harder to resist than the forbidden fruit. The wretched child feels that the hunger tormenting him will continue to torment him forever, and that his stomach is a bottomless pit. He has already swallowed two hundred grams, and again he must struggle against the temptation. And although logic warns him of the terrible results – he doesn't care, he gives in! How can he find the willpower when the small 100-gram portion is driving him crazy, pulling at him like a magnet? Strange ideas buzz through his miserable brain, the sweet aroma of the bread tingles in his nostrils. The wild cry of hunger overwhelms the boy, and he grabs the remainder of the dry bread and quickly devours it, choking with each bite. In a frightening voice, filled with bitterness and venom, logic demands: "And what will you do tomorrow without bread? Tomorrow! Tomorrow!" "Do I have a tomorrow?" the despairing child thinks. His common sense presents Eli with an even more difficult question:

Tomorrow is tomorrow, but what about the day after tomorrow, you confused child!" I was hungry, the child explains in the imaginary dialogue. "That's no reason. Do you want to be like your neighbor, Oppenheim? The child conjures up the sight of a walking corpse, skin and bones, his eye sockets empty and dead. No! No! A voice inside him cries. I don't want to die, I want to live, I want to say alive after the war too. "Back to work, the breakfast break is over," the foreman yells. "Take your plane and start working!" Eli rolls up his sleeve and begins polishing a beam.

The sun suddenly pierces the dark, heavy clouds, its rays lighting up the room. Little Eli quietly enjoys the light that floods his anguished soul...The clock strikes two when Eli returns home. On the staircase, his neighbor Oppenheim opens his apartment door a crack. Through the narrow opening, Eli sees the horrible face of the walking-dead. "Hello, Beigelman," Oppenheim stammers, swallowing his saliva. "Any n-n-n-new rations in the city?" "No, nothing new," Eli replies softly, without taking his eyes off the man. "I can't go on fasting like this any more," says Oppenheim, shocked by the boy's reply. "I finished my bread a long time ago. If you have a drop of coffee, I'd be glad to fill my belly with some." Eli shrugs his shoulders and goes into his apartment. Even before he passes the threshold, he's welcomed by confused words: "Eli, we've got one coupon for a carrot, a radish and some parsley. Take it and run! You know how it is, maybe in another minute...Please," Shura, agitated, pleads with him, urging him to go at once...

Every day Eli goes to work, and every day, when he returns home, he finds his mother in front of the awful stove, blowing on the flames like a dragon. None of those warm kisses on his forehead she used to welcome him with before the war. Only poverty greets him every day, poverty that gives off a terrible stench, poverty full of acrid smoke, accursed poverty! "*A schwartz tzebrochene geta leben!*" –

black, broken ghetto life – Eli's mother swears as she raises her soot-covered face; I've already brought three maintenance men but they don't understand anything. They just made the stove worse. The maintenance service only works for people with connections. That's how it is, my son, these are the times we live in. Will we ever live to see better times? Only God knows. All we know now is poverty, hunger, cold, and many, many other troubles. The only time I feel happy is when I lie down to sleep. Every day that passes is a victory for us, my son. It's a good thing that I don't work far away. That would kill me altogether," Shura says, and plods over to her bed, breathing heavily, her body bent over. She drops on to the sheets like a log, and rests. "What's new, my son?" "Ah, Momma, if only you knew! Soon all of us will get a new ration, a special ration." "Go on, go on," the mother cries excitedly, "I feel my last bit of strength draining out of me." In a festive, reverberating voice, Eli enumerates all the items that will be in the ration, and poor Shura begins to shake all over. "It's surely not for us, but for the rich, for our accursed Beirat." "No, Mama! Eli cries excitedly, this ration will be for us." "If only that were true. We'll see. And what news have you brought?" Shura asks. "On Utrzednicza St. near the barbed wire they shot a young man, no one knows why." "Is he dead?" Shura asks. "Yes," Eli replies in a soft voice. "Oy vey," Shura moans under her breath. "What a dog's life. Who would have believed, my son, that you, I and Benitza would go through such a horrible time! And to think that all of our suffering may be for nothing. That we may just disappear, swallowed up in this hell. All this work for nothing, all these illusions in vain! Even our own brethren are sucking our blood, making our suffering worse and causing us to weep bitterly. And that awful old man, that accursed Rumkowski, who starves us in this chicken coop of his and sends us by the thousands to the Marysin cemetery. He'd better be careful," Shura cries aloud angrily, making a fist with her scrawny hand.

"What did you eat today, Eli" She asks. "The usual, Momma, soup with six or seven pieces of potato." "The swine," she reacts with fury. "They leave the noodles and potatoes for themselves, and for the small fry, like us, nothing! That's how it is, my son. They all live on our backs. The Beirat takes tons of food for themselves. They get so much oil and extra rations. They drink our blood like vampires. And the weak and sick disappear without leaving a trace. Even those who still feel all right get sick in the end, because hunger causes tuberculosis and thousands of other diseases. And finally, we all end up in the cemetery, wrapped in a layer of black, rough earth instead of shrouds. That's it, that's our life. Just that," Shura mutters, and adds in a whisper: "Eli, cover the window." The boy covers the pane with a black scarf, and then leaps back onto the floor. Outside a storm is gathering, alternately blustering and growing weaker. Sometimes it bursts forth with a satanic laugh, or at least that's how it seems to Eli, who thinks of the storm's moans as voices from beyond the grave, songs from hell, birds predicting a catastrophe. On the stove, a soup-like liquid is boiling in a blue pot. Bits of grated turnip dance between tiny flakes of potato. Eli constantly lifts the pot to check the bottom. Then he fries some flour in a pan, and pours it into the soup. "Let's all go to the table," he says quietly. Shura drags herself out of the bed and serves the thin white liquid to her son and daughter. They eat. Their noses run, their foreheads sweat. On their cheeks, for a brief moment, a red flush blooms.

Benitza is Ill

Benitza is fading before their eyes. Her skin is grayish. The goodness and simplicity of an angel shine from her blue eyes. She lies in her corner, and her gaze, filled with love and innocence, passes slowly over the room. The small child's body is spent. Every noise shakes the agitated heart inside that fragile body. So gentle, she does not dare reveal her suffering to her mother. Her birdlike appetite has enabled her to adjust to the life of the ghetto. Despite her poor health, she is not sad. Nor is she cheerful, but from time to time her face glows. Shura, worried, has decided to call a doctor, who has finally given in to her entreaties and agreed to come to see the patient. The little girl allows him to examine her, and patiently bears the touch of his cold, thick fingers. With frigid eyes, the doctor is lost in gloomy thoughts. But suddenly he breaks the silence: "The situation is grave, Mrs. Beigelman, an x-ray is urgently needed, because my examination is not sufficient. The little one must absolutely not exert herself, because her heart is very weak. And as for food, he says, with a deep sigh, feed her with a teaspoon, constantly. I know the conditions are not good, but health pays no heed to such arguments, right?" He sits at the table, prescribes several medications, and rolls up his sleeve a bit to see what time it is. "Five minutes to twelve," he says impatiently, "I should have been at the hospital long ago. Ah, how fast time passes." He takes his doctor's hat and his bag, and hurries to the door.

After the doctor goes, Shura is alone again with her dreary thoughts. What's the point of bringing a specialist, when that only increases the uncertainty. When all is said and done, I don't know what's wrong with her. Damn those doctors who don't know anything. She curses the life of the ghetto, goes over to her daughter's bed and caresses her black hair. Benitza turns a love-filled gaze at her mother, and a pale smile of suffering spreads over her face.

Eli Loses his Cap

…In the meantime, the nasty old lady is brazenly playing with the boy's cap He is so furious he dares to do something even more brazen. With both hands, he grabs hold of the detestable foot to wrest his cap free…

After this terrible incident, the din grows louder and the storm roars harder. The problem of the cap is still unsolved; it's even more complicated, because the forest of nervous feet continues on its way uninterrupted. In desperation, Eli reaches out to try to regain his property, and when he straightens up, he yells into the stout woman's ear: "Lady, move your fat pole! Oh, God, are you deaf? Your foot is on my hat!" But the woman screeches, waving her ration coupons like a madwoman.

Now Eli is crawling on all fours, trying to salvage his cap. Suddenly someone unintentionally sits down on his skeletal back. Under all that weight, the boy is mercilessly crushed to the ground. His nose smashes against the floor. He sees stars. Rubbing his painful bruise, he goes on tirelessly searching…

Suddenly he sees a dark object. My hat! He cries joyously, and puts out his hand to grab the object he wants so badly. Just then, the woman's foot moves sharply, and with her clog she crushes the most vulnerable finger on the poor boy's right hand. "*Oi, vey!* Eli screams with pain. "*Oi, vey!*" he yells again, so loud that all the passersby freeze on the spot. "*Ver shreit azoy?*[10]" they all call out. The cruel clog slides a little sideways and frees the poor boy's finger. "*A brokh af im,*[11]" he cries out with relief. He straightens

[10] Yiddish: "Who's yelling like that?"
[11] Yiddish: "A curse upon his head"

45

up at once, but then his head accidentally bangs against a boy whose nose is as red as a tomato. Luckily, that boy, fuming with pain and anger, is called just then to the cashier.

Eli looks at the bleak co-op, swarming with ghosts. How hard it is to stand in line! But the hunger in these empty bellies wins out, even if the compensation, at the end of the wait, is really paltry. When there are no nightingales around, you can even think of a crow as a songbird. How apt this expression is to the wretched poverty of the ghetto!

Eli is only a drop in this sea. His hat has flown away and he's boiling mad. He was close to the window when the damn hat…how will he find it now, in this stormy sea? His body is bent in two, and he looks in desperation through the tumult of feet moving in every direction. Then suddenly, it seems to him that there, between that woman's feet…

Red with anger and dripping sweat, he deliberately trips the woman, who screams, and falls face forward into the crowd. Eli grabs the desired object. But, no! It's not the hat, only a filthy apron. He is beside himself with rage and bitterness, and once again has no idea where to turn. "Boy," a voice rings out, "your cap's over there, on the stove!" It was the voice of the woman who had stumbled because of him just a minute ago. "You don't have to make such a fuss," she says. "And you've bruised my face too!" The boy with the red nose yells, and disappears at once into the sea of heads. Eli stuffs his cap deep inside his torn coat pocket, to make sure he doesn't lose it again. He wants to take out his coupons. What a disaster! The pocket is empty. He shakes out the tattered coat. Nothing! He pales, reddens and bursts like a madman into the crowd. Curses fall upon him from all sides. He doesn't reply, only goes on searching. This is the very worst...the frantic boy thinks, and crawling through the forest of feet, he goes on looking. But his search ends in disappointment. White as a sheet, he nervously feels around in his clothing. But that does no good. He lowers his eyes. Finally! In one of his yellow clogs he sees the coupons. Dizzy with joy, light as a feather, he dives into the human whirlpool, his head forward, waving his cherished coupons. "Get that kid out of here!" a woman selling vegetables shouts. Her eyes are small, alert and suspicious and she menacingly points a finger at Eli...

The boy is already approaching his objective. But suddenly he hears a voice, which, strangely enough, sounds familiar. The pleading eyes of his neighbor, Oppenheim, lock onto his face. The boy hesitates..."Give me your coupon," Eli whispers, and Oppenheim extends his scrawny hand. A fist appears from nowhere and smacks Oppenheim's arm. The coupon flies up in the air. The miserable skeleton wobbles and then collapses onto the floor like a felled tree..."Careful!" someone calls out, "you'll trample him." Eli leaves the line, and with the help of some others, pulls the human wreckage out of danger. But before he can put Oppenheim back on his feet, the man starts shaking again. Eli leans his neighbor against the wall. The living-dead man moans quietly. The boy takes his coupon from him, and like a swift arrow, he throws himself into the line. He arrives just in time...he hands over his coupon and Oppenheim's...and a quarter of an hour later, a carrot and parsley soup is bubbling on the stove.

Oppenheim's Story

Oppenheim's life is even more piteous than the Beigelman family's. He's in a desperate state, and the only way out for him is suicide. The life force has been extinguished in him. He has lost touch with reality. Who is this man? A man who is all alone, who was among the first Jews to be transferred to the ghetto. The specter of death terrifies him. Suffering has made him frighteningly emaciated. Hunger has wreaked havoc on this man, who was once a real glutton. His mind is confused. He no longer divides his bread into portions, as he used to do, but swallows it all in two or three days, and fasts the rest of the week. He has lost all desire or human feeling, and in a short while has turned into a walking corpse. Let's not mince words: his room is a wretched lair... He has cut up all the furniture and uses it as wood for heating. Only his bed, on which he lays his fragile body, has remained whole.

Oppenheim, who used to be an expert at elbowing his way through every line, has become a skeletal creature, shy and stammering. He takes his place at the end of the line, and as soon as he gets home, he devours his whole ration at one go. Such a confused life could not help but strike a fatal blow to this man with his stormy temperament. There's no point in looking for someone higher up to support him, who would want to help that scarecrow wearing that foolish, expressionless mask? That's all you can say about the man. A person haunted by hunger and relentless delusions that are slowly killing him. His dry cough sometimes disturbs Eli's sleep, and infuriated, the boy curses his neighbor. Shura seems indifferent to these

49

daily concerts, which to her are part of the dreary life of the ghetto. Often, when Oppenheim's cough becomes truly unbearable, she listens and utters black prophecies. "Here's one more going kaput! Another dead one for Rumkowski! That's how it is, my little Eli: there are those who eat like gluttons, and hundreds of others who suffer." And when she feels a trace of pity for their neighbor, Eli listens. "How he coughs!" he says to his mother. "From the frying pan into the fire," she replies and goes on chewing a piece of turnip. "It won't be long before he too ends up in the Marysin cemetery." "There won't be anyone to cry at his grave," the boy whispers. "Yes, and no one to put up a tombstone," Shura answers. "He's so pitiful," Eli cries out, full of compassion, "All he knows is poverty and sorrow." "He's not the only one. Thousands of us are broken and shattered, and we all deserve some compassion," Shura says defensively. "But he has no one. No one to say a good word to him. No one to stand in his place in the lines and at the stores. Mama, I'm going to visit him, maybe he wants some coffee. I'll bring him a cup." "Go, if you want to," Shura says apathetically. "It definitely won't be sad at his place!"

Eli goes out to the stairs and opens his neighbor's creaking door. He doesn't even hear the familiar voice asking "Ver iz dos?"[12] Oppenheim has no reason to be afraid of thieves, he's already devoured his rations long ago, and the only thing he can generously offer robbers is pure poverty. The boy surprises the recluse in his bed, wound up like a spring, indifferent to the world around him. "How are you neighbor?" Eli asks. Oppenheim, breathing hard and

[12] Yiddish: "Who is it?"

groaning, turns his head towards the boy. Eli draws back when he sees the wretched man's face. His eyes are expressionless, like deep, vacant pits, no longer looking anywhere. "I, I..," Oppenheim begins speaking with difficulty, "I don't know myself how I am, but I feel I don't have much time left." "Are you hungry?" Eli asks. "Hungry?" Oppenheim pronounces the word slowly. "Nooo, not at all, on the contrary, food disgusts me." "That's no good, you'll drop of exhaustion." Oppenheim pays no attention to Eli's words, and mutters: "How good it is not to be hungry." "Maybe you'd like some coffee?" Eli asks. "Coffee?" the sick man is astonished, not understanding the meaning of Eli's offer. "Coffee, oh, coffee, no I don't need coffee." "Then what do you need?" "I...I don't need anything anymore." "Goodbye for now, Oppenheim," Eli says in a low voice and tiptoes out of the lair.

When he returns home, his mother asks grudgingly: "How's our sick neighbor?" "Kaput, Mama, he's like death." "I knew he was getting worse," Shura says with a heavy sigh.

The Marysin Cemetery

The next day, when Eli climbs the narrow wooden steps of
the building, he hears Oppenheim's faint voice in the hallway. He stops for a minute, although he's anxious to get
home because his stomach is rumbling relentlessly. He
hears another moan. I'm going there, Eli says to himself,
and at once he opens the creaking door. The room is as
filthy and wretched as ever, but its tenant's condition has
grown even worse. Since he doesn't have a chamber pot, he
relieves himself on the floor, and there, next to the bed, is
a disgusting puddle of a green, blood-stained liquid. Eli
shudders. He's just noticed a drizzle of excrement dripping
from the sheet onto the soiled floor. He's afraid to draw
closer. Standing motionless as a statue, he looks at this horrific scene of misery.

"Little one," Oppenheim begins in a trembling voice. "I
have a very special request to make of you. As you can see,
these are my last hours. I'll die forgotten and be buried like
a dead dog, without a ceremony. I don't know if it will be
easy for you, but you have a good heart, and you won't be
able to refuse my last request. My son, after my death,
which is inevitable, go to the burial society and order a
small memorial plaque with my first name, my last name,
the date of my birth and of my death." "Don't talk
nonsense," Eli responds, "don't think about death. You
have to live and believe in God." The only reply is a groan.
Oppenheim is clearly suffering terribly; his marble-like
face is constricted and twitching horribly. Eli is frightened
by the sight, and draws back silently. Oppenheim's body
curls up into a ball and then freezes in a position of pain.

He's dead, Eli suddenly thinks, and is seized by awful fright at the sight of the emaciated, still body. He runs home. "What do you think you are, the Kriminalpolizei? What happened?" Shura asks anxiously. "Mama, our neighbor Oppenheim is lying on his mattress and looks like a corpse. I think he's dead." "That's not surprising. How do you expect a man like him to live on Rumkowski's rations? You have to remember that before the war he was a real glutton," the mother begins to tell him. "But, Mama, he can't look at food anymore!" "That's a bad sign. I don't think our neighbor can live much longer," Shura says and sticks her knife into a yellow turnip.

At night, Oppenheim's lungs hemorrhage, and before he can be taken to the hospital, he dies. Before the war, an event like that would surely have shocked the tenants of the building, but now, such a death is just an everyday occurrence.

At the entrance to the building, a small black wagon that serves as a hearse stands harnessed to an old, skinny horse with fading eyes. It's the start of winter, and a heavy snow has fallen at night. The lamp on the gloomy entrance casts a trembling shadow on the cracked wall. Its light produces a sharp angle illuminating half of the wagon and half of the driver's face. The silence of death pervades everything, a terrifying wind is blowing, and snowflakes sparkling like diamonds hover in the darkness. Two men come out of the building, carrying a narrow board on which there is a body covered with a white sheet. The heavy skull swings with each movement the porters make. The snow under their feet makes a squeaking sound. They place the wooden board and the body on the wagon, and a moment later, they are sitting on the bench. With a lash of his whip, the driver urges the horses to move, and the small carriage quickly slides over the fresh, shining snow. The drama that has just taken place is the daily bread and butter of the ghetto's undertakers.

The building is sunk in a deep sleep, but when the pale dawn rends the darkness of the night, the tenants know Oppenheim is dead. Some feel pity for him, others react with indifference, yet others predict the same tragic end for all of them.

Oppenheim has died and now the boy is agonizing over his sense of guilt. The wretched man's fragmented sentences still ring in his ears. Do this for me, you have a good heart. The voice is so clear that Eli looks around the room in alarm. "What's wrong with you?" his mother asks, noticing his strange, morose behavior. "Nothing, Mama," Eli replies, shamefacedly. I won't say anything to Mama, Eli thinks, and tries to drive away the voice that is upsetting him, while he helps his mother split the logs. A white, powdery snow is falling soundlessly outside the window. Perhaps it's better for him now that he's dead, no, it's a sin to think that everyone has the right to live. But is it really worth the effort? Life is a huge vale of tears, isn't that so? Eli is tormented: should he fulfill the dead man's last wish or not? It seems to him that in his conscience he hears the lashing of a whip. The last wish of a dying man is sacred, and since it's been left in your hands, you are obliged to fulfill it. If not, woe to you, you're a sinner! Eli shuts his eyes tightly, frightened by the voice of God.

At night he has a strange dream. Oppenheim appears to him, weeping bitter tears and urging him to carry out his only request. Eli sits up straight in bed, shakes his mother awake and screams in fright: "Mama, Mama!" "What hap-

55

pened?" Shura, awakening, cries out. "No! no!" the boy moans through his bluish lips and his head falls back weakly on the pillow. "Why are you waking me up in the middle of the night if nothing's wrong?" "I had a dream, Mama, I dreamt," he mutters feebly, as his lids close.

More and more death wagons are now going through the streets of the dying ghetto. Death, so cruel and indifferent, is reaping victims with growing force. Every day Eli sees scenes of dreadful suffering, every day he hears heart-rending cries of relatives mourning the death of their loved ones. Poor Eli witnesses horrifying pictures that make his head whirl.

Hearses and bodies, bodies and hearses swirl wildly in his imagination. From time to time, Oppenheim's face appears and God's voice commands: 'Woe to you if you do not fulfill the dead man's wish.' Eli can only think of God as an awesome, frightening figure. The influence of the rabbis has left a destructive imprint on the boy's soul. In his eyes, God is a fearful power, who for any sin, even the slightest, is liable to cast him into Hell. But the ghetto itself is hell, isn't it? Eli asks in complete seriousness. Perhaps Rumkowski is really Satan incarnate? No, a Jew cannot be Satan. A Gentile, perhaps, but a Jew, no. Satan is neither a Jew nor a Gentile, he's Satan and that's it.

These are the mystical byways in which Eli's sick soul wanders. The boy is immersed in the forty-nine gates of horror of the ghetto. His nights are troubled, the thoughts that haunt him by day return to plague him at night, a jumble of ghostly pictures. Eli falls asleep, listening distractedly with one ear to the mysterious, ghastly cries of the storm.

But the dead man's voice gives him no rest. He finally

decides to go to the office of the burial society to fulfill Oppenheim's last wish. The skies are leaden, the streets are frozen, the wind is blustering. The snow-covered plots of Marysin lie before the solitary boy. From time to time, a strong wind blows searing snowflakes into Eli's blue face. His head is sunk into a large collar, only his nose and his frightened eyes peeping out of it.

Eli begins to walk on the dirt path that leads to the cemetery. Terrified, he walks without looking around him. Majestic trees, which in spring and summer wear coats of splendid foliage, are silent now, naked. In the summer, Eli likes to listen to the cheerful rustling of their leaves, but today they seem to have been struck dumb. Poor trees, he thinks, but they at least have some hope, while we, Almighty God, are marching towards certain oblivion. The branches of the trees shake with cold, despairing, as mute as the grave. Eli wonders, do our travails also obey the laws of nature?

It's no wonder that the boy poses such questions to himself. Life has made him old before his time. His soul inclines towards mysticism and does not permit logic to guide him. Often his thoughts are not those of a child. His feelings are loftier than those of an adult Unfortunately, there is no longer anyone who will see to his future education.

The frozen earth squeaks under Eli's feet, groaning with pain. The storm whips at his face. Everything twists and turns, storming under his gaze, and ideas flow towards him, like the snow-covered horizon. Between the moans of the wind, Eli hears a deep voice and the whisk of a whip at his back. He jumps into the side of the road. A small, black hearse swiftly passes him by. The taste of death emanates from that box on wheels. A quarter of an hour later, a man asks him the way to the cemetery. Eli looks him over from head to toe. He must be new around here or a stranger, because everyone in the ghetto knows the way to the cemetery. But since he's not familiar with this dreary place, Eli will show him. He reaches out his skinny arm, and then two more figures appear behind the man – a mother and daughter desperately holding on to one another, plodding towards Marysin: "*Oy, vey, mein Gott!*" the woman cries in a broken voice, "*Mein Yossele, mein Yossele!*[14] How could you have left this world? So young and so ill-fated! Oh, when will this suffering come to an end? Oh, I'll never forget you. I want to die. Do you hear me? I want to be where my son is." She reaches out her arm in the direction of the cemetery entrance and then clenches her fingers. The curly-haired girl casts a dull gaze at the snow-covered plain. They move on, and Eli accompanies them. Then the boy passes the two forlorn women and enters the cemetery.

Ancient, leaning tombstones covered with snow dot the field. Some others, not as old, still stand upright. In the end, they'll all collapse, Eli thinks, as he turns his melancholy gaze to the crumbling gravestones. How powerful time is! It erases the most painful memories, dries the bitterest of tears, and destroys the proudest monuments! He touches the marble of a tombstone and then passes his finger over the cracks and broken bits of the stone, the traces of destructive time. There are numerous paths in front of the boy. Lost in his mystical thoughts, Eli begins walking along a very narrow path, between two vertical tombstones. Occasionally, he becomes entangled

[14] Yiddish: "Oh, God! My Yossele, my Yossele!"

in the snow-covered branch of a bush, but he is indifferent to these kisses of frost. First names and family names march in disorder in front of his eyes. Shmuel Rosen, 24 years old. Ah, what a fine age, Eli thinks. Irena Donskah, our beloved daughter. Golden letters decorate the opulent tombstones of the rich who passed away before the war. In the distance, above a forest of memorial tablets, large and small, arises the magnificent dome of the wealthy Poznansky family's mausoleum. The farther he goes into the cemetery, the poorer the tombstones become, and at the very end, he sees the crooked inscriptions of the ghetto's dead. These ugly, wretched plaques vividly exude their suffering. One need only glance at them to understand the tragic story of the Litzmannstadt Ghetto: dead men and women aged twenty two, eighteen, nineteen, three months, a month! God, Eli whispers. How could you take such young lives? A man is repairing a memorial plaque on one of the graves. A little farther away, at the foot of another small grave, a solitary woman lies, wrapped in a shawl. She is caressing and kissing the snow-covered ground with her blue lips. "*Mein kind*"[15] she sobs, and the edge of her mourning veil suddenly flies up and chokes her cry…Eli turns away from this touching sight and begins to walk on the path leading to the house of the burial society.

He climbs the stairs of the lavish building and opens the door of the morgue, which gives off the scent of corpses. How quiet it is, and how terrible, he thinks, and his eyes take in a black coffin with white candles lit above it. His steps echo throughout the large chamber. On stretchers close to the coffin lie bodies wrapped in white shrouds. A

[15] Yiddish: "My child."

woman, still young, is tearing the hair from her head with her fists and racing around madly inside the room. Eli flees from this terrible place and goes into the waiting room. There too only dread prevails. Workers holding spades in their hands sit on the benches conversing. Eli expresses his request and pays…with the money from Oppenheim's pension after he is promised that the inscription will be engraved on the stone in two days. He returns home, calm and satisfied, and now that he has fulfilled the gloomy wish of his dead neighbor, he feels he deserves some show of gratitude from the omnipotent God.

The Carpentry Shop Canteen

Precisely at 12 noon – such style! - a metallic ring announces the lunch break. The courtyard of the carpentry shop fills up at once with workers, dashing about and holding their food bowls in their hands. Mr. Eliezer places a stool he has just finished on top of a pile of beams, grabs his bowl and races towards the canteen. Little Eli's heart jumps with joy. The boy leaps through the window into the courtyard, waving his bowl, and flies like an arrow. When he arrives, huffing and puffing, in front of the kitchen, which is emitting huge clouds of steam, he asks himself which serving counter he should choose.

Right next to him there's a man who has just received his portion and is angrily stirring the soup with his spoon. "What happened?" The troubled boy asks. "She hardly gave me any potatoes, *a brokh zol ir trefen*[16] ," he curses the woman with the ladle and goes back to stirring the thin liquid under Eli's nose. "Hmmm…that's right, there really isn't much here," the boy says and suggests the man go and complain. The man hesitates a moment, and then gnashing his teeth, he elbows his way through the crowd and goes up to the counter. With a despairing look on his face, he shows the woman the contents of his bowl. "Madam," he opens in a whining voice, "I didn't get my two hundred grams of potatoes." "Give me your bowl," the fat woman shouts in a threatening voice and reaches out her hand. She pours the soup from the bowl into the ladle and then back from the ladle into the bowl, and carefully scrutinizes each piece of potato. "One, two, three, four, five, six!" the dry,

---

[16] A curse upon you!

61

cold voice of the woman at the counter roars, "now leave me in peace." "*Oy vey!*" the poor man cries out, "I'm a dog if there are two hundred grams of potatoes here! Wait until we meet after the war...," he adds in anger, and walks away, as he continues furiously stirring his thin soup. "Hey!" a worker passing by him calls out, "don't bang your bowl so hard, you're liable to make a hole in it!"

In the meantime, Eli gets to the counter. He hands his lunch coupon to the supervisor who stamps it, and the bowl to the woman who serves the food. She dawdles, and then dips the ladle into the full pot. Eli stands on his tiptoes watching attentively to see how the fat woman is cheating him. "Go a little deeper," the boy groans bitterly. "No one gets to bargain here!" she screeches, and skillfully maneuvers the ladle so that on the way it drops several pieces of potato. "But you're dropping a lot of potatoes back into the pot!" the despairing child cries out. "I won't give you more than two hundred grams, you ragamuffin!"

Just then, a young man, wearing high boots and carrying a briefcase in one hand and his bowl in the other, comes up to the counter without standing in line. "Oh, hello, sir," the woman says, all smiles, and takes the bowl from his hand. Then she dips the ladle deep inside the pot, and serves him a ladle full of potatoes. Without saying a word, the man covers his bowl with an improvised cover and walks away rapidly. "He gets a kilo of potatoes, and I get this watery juice," Eli sobs in vain. He hurls curses he didn't even know he knew at the nasty woman and takes back his bowl.

Eli No Longer Goes to Work

Hunger has turned Eli into a small walking corpse, amusing himself and leading a wretched life at one and the same time. Very soon, the boy becomes unfit to work. Such stupidity, to place any trade or a saw in those small, emaciated hands! They shake all the time, and after a few minutes of effort, they drop whatever tools they're holding. In the eyes of the foreman, Eli is an idler, a schlemiel and a professional shirker.

When poor Eli hears his supervisors' authoritative shouts from afar, he cowers among the beams of wood and his body trembles as if he were a frightened puppy.

Within a short time, the other workers begin to regard him as a nuisance. Some of them complain that he's always underfoot, and if that wasn't bad enough, one day Eli distractedly steps on a saw, which breaks with a loud cracking sound. The furious foreman grabs the boy by his collar and sends him into the hallway with a kick. That same day, everyone seems to be looking for a pretext to harass the boy. The social worker invites Eli for a talk. She's already heard about him, and doesn't make much of an effort to look into his case. She poses a few short questions to him, which he answers under his breath. After a fifteen-minute interview, she assigns him to a place where the work is hard and the machines make an infernal racket. Everyone always provoking him and sending him from place to place. Eli looks with dazed eyes at the workers who are dispatching him this way and that and doesn't always understand what they want of him. He grows even skinnier, and it tears his suffering mother's heart when he

63

confides his troubles to her. Shura heaps curses on her son's hangmen. Eli's short legs are so thin they can hardly carry his strange body. When Shura sees her son losing weight from one minute to the next, she forbids him to go back to work and puts him to bed.

As he lies in bed from morning to night, Eli thinks about his bizarre experience in Marysin. His mother makes him some flour soup – *meil soupe* – and he gulps it down and licks his lips. "After the war," Shura says, you'll see what I'll do to those bastards. I'll start with the foreman. With my own hands, I'll hang him from a tree. What does he think, that this war will go on forever and he can torment you endlessly? He'd better be careful!" She goes on, clenching her fists, "Before the war, he sold stockings in the street, and now he thinks he's a king. And you, don't you get sick on me now! And to think that I've nothing substantial to give you to eat!" She bends down to her son and kisses him on the forehead, as she used to do before the war. Then she adds with determination, "We'll survive. We'll get through this ghetto alive, right, my precious one?" Eli, moved by his mother's kiss, falls into a deep, sweet sleep.

Eli is burning up with fever. He thrashes about as if someone is torturing him, finding it hard to move his feverish lips and muttering strange half sentences. "I put a memorial plaque on the grave. God will bless me. In time, everything will become peaceful, because time has so much power…" These were the confused words being uttered by the small patient. Her face twisted with pain, Shura walks over to her son and removes the thermometer from under his armpit. "Forty!" she cries out in alarm, and grabs her head with her hands. She quickly throws her blue coat over her shoulders and runs outside…

The doctor lives nearby. Shura prefers a private visit, even if it costs her dearly. On the gleaming clinic door, there's a small sign announcing the hours of reception and visits. With a pounding heart, she knocks on the door. A tall blonde with painted lips opens it and asks dryly: "Who are you looking for?" The doctor? What, are you blind, or don't you know how to read? The doctor only receives at the hours shown here." "But my son has a high fever. Isn't that dangerous? So I thought perhaps the doctor would come," Shura insists. The doctor's wife has no time for unnecessary politeness. She angrily slams the door in Shura's face. *A brokh*! Shura curses. Who does she think she is, that *beiratinka*[17] Just you wait, Missus, I'll burn you in my bonfire too!

Whether she likes it or not, Shura has to obey the rules. That evening the doctor comes to the Beigelmans' room. Standing at the threshold, he already begins choking from the mixture of putrid smells that fills the room. "It's impossible to breathe the air here! How can you live in this stench? You'll kill the sick boy!" The doctor scolds white-faced Shura. "But, doctor, we live in dreadful conditions." "We all live in the same conditions," the doctor replies dryly, but he doesn't dare persist because he's ashamed of his blatant lie. "Dear God, can't you open the window and straighten up your apartment a bit? If I had known, I wouldn't have stepped foot in this place. The boy is getting really good treatment," the doctor goes on in a mocking tone, as he looks for a place to put down his bag and hat. After he arranges his instruments on the

[17] Yiddish: privileged (the female form of beirat).

65

windowsill, Shura moves away so as not to interfere with his examination. "Fine, now let's examine our patient," the doctor says, putting on his stethoscope. Shura anxiously watches the doctor's face as he concentrates on his examination. With his brow furrowed, and his gaze fixed on a corner of the room, he muses. The tiny wrinkles in his forehead give no hint of his diagnosis. He asks the patient to sit up straight, and examines him carefully. Shura doesn't take her eyes off him, as if he were God, and tries to guess the truth based on the movements of his facial muscles. The doctor stands up and gives the mother his dreadful news: "Your son is suffering from tuberculosis in the initial stage, but his condition is not hopeless. You have to make an effort to give him more nutritious food, especially sugar. He must have lots of it. Try to get some butter too. In short, do whatever you can to save him, and don't scrimp on fats." Shura wrings her hands and turns a pleading gaze at the doctor. "But dear God, where will I find butter? With what money?" she mutters bitterly. "Don't despair. Tell yourself it's only the beginning. I'll give you a coupon for the *Diet Laden*.[18] The main thing is to keep your spirits up." He sits by the window, takes out a notebook, writes several prescriptions and the coupon he promised. Shura, paler than death, looks affectionately at her beloved son. She can only see his small, feverish face. The doctor speaks one more word of warning: the closed, dirty air in the room is likely to harm her son's weak lungs.

Following the doctor's advice, Shura straightens up the room a bit...

She must save her son, even at the cost of her own

[18] German: Co-op for special nutrition.

health. Her cheeks become more and more sunken, and the wrinkles in her coarse face grow more numerous. She constantly hovers around her son's bed, trying to sweeten his life with a few tender words. She tries to strengthen his little body with sugar and butter she has obtained with the last of her money. The boy hallucinates, allowing his feverish imagination to take him on mysterious paths.

In the evening, when the storm is raging in the chimney and behind the window, Eli dreams about the Marysin cemetery. He recalls his experience intensely, in fragmented, confused sentences. "Mama! I went there in an awful snowstorm. I was happy, because I was serving the dead man and God. How do you get to the cemetery? Walk straight ahead, straight ahead. There are lots and lots of graves there. Time has so much power, it destroys the tombstones as if they were toys, it heals the deepest wounds," the boy mutters through his feverish lips. "Mama!" he yells suddenly, and sits up straight. "If so many people die, can that happen to me too?"

His eyes burn like flaming coals, and dreadful chills shake his whole body. With tear-filled eyes, Shura lays her stringy hand on her son's head and gently soothes him: "Shh, shh, my little one. Relax, my precious one! These attacks make you sicker." Eli holds on to her rough hand and touches it with his lips. A few minutes later, he lays his head on the pillow and falls asleep, breathing deeply.

Weeks go by like that. Eli still has a fever, and Shura's heart overflows with grief. The doctor's second visit only increases her sorrow. The patient's condition is worsening. Like a madwoman, Shura dashes from store to store, and with the last groschen she's earned through her hard labor she buys several grams of butter. On more than one occasion, someone cheats her. She has more than her share of suffering but she struggles like a ship in a stormy sea.

She denies herself everything she can – calculating, planning, slowly ruining her own health. The thought that she might save her son through her desperate efforts strengthens her grim faith. After the doctor's visit, Eli's appetite seems to be increasing, but very soon he again loses any desire to eat, and his poor mother despairs. "Why don't you want to eat, my darling? Can't you see I'm giving my life and my blood so you'll get well again. Don't you appreciate what I'm doing? *Oy vey*! What will I do with you?" The mercury in the thermometer jumps – once up and once down. When the silver column in the tube rises, the mother's heart beats doubly fast and her breath stops. When the mercury goes down a bit, her heart jumps with joy, like that of a child. Eli then becomes fully conscious, and Shura whispers words of affection to him, so he will feel her motherly love and know that someone is taking care of him.

The nights are stormy, blustering with snow and wind. In the snow-covered ghetto, the storm rages like the devil. Above the houses, the clouds wrestle angrily. The snow gyrates wildly like a top in the streets to the sound of the distant shrieks of wind. The silent windows lie frigid under a layer of frost. The ghetto sleeps. Nature gives free rein to its forces. The storm brings with it large clumps of snow and hurls them at the walls of the houses, where they shatter and die. But new clouds, even more menacing, are already gathering in the sky. Everything twirls, turning around some hellish axis. In the distance, a shutter slams shut, a drainpipe squeaks. Heaps of snow adorn the winding streets of the small ghetto, turning it into a desert of white dunes. The gusty winds battle with one another like goring bulls. The street lamps waver like ghosts, trembling in the fierce winds. They shriek with a menacing sound, as if they were cursing frenzied nature.

That night, Shura suffers the torments of hell. She sits at her son's bed, arranging the pillows behind his head, caressing his purplish face and praying ardently. The boy is hallucinating. From time to time, he sits up suddenly, screams, threatens, and immediately falls back, exhausted, gravely alarming his mother, who freezes, motionless. When she lays her hand on his forehead, she feels she is putting it into a fire. The small electric bulb gives off a miserly light. The room is dark, and the silence of death hovers over it. Only Eli's fragmentary sentences break the silence from time to time. "*Mein kind*, be calm. Don't you know me? I'm your mother." Eli, groggy, barely conscious, looks at Shura's face but keeps on hallucinating. Suddenly, he sits up and whispers: "What's that there in the corner? Yes, there," and he fixes his wide-open eyes on a specific point. "That's nothing, my child. It's a broom." "Mama," the panic-stricken boy cries out, his eyes drawn into slits, "That's death looking at me. He wants to hypnotize me. Help!" he screams, and then drops his head at once onto the pillow.

Outside, the storm rages, quiets down and then howls again. The mother and son listen to the shrieks of the wind. She – conscious and miserable – he, bewildered and apathetic. Beset by anxiety, she asks herself, what should I do? No one will come to the house at this hour, but still, I can't leave him alone in this condition. Definitely not. Unless…I'll lock the door and run to the hospital or to the doctor. Oh, God, God! What should I do? Run fast! Be brave! Do something! An inner voice calls out to her.

Shura throws her coat on her shrunken body, kisses her son, and runs out. In the street, the frenzied storm lifts her as if they were locked in a satanic dance. Hah, ha, ha! the devil bursts into a hellish cackle, dragging behind him an enormous white cloud. With a frightful noise, a roof tile shatters on the cobblestones. At the corner of the street, a lamp sways to and fro. Circles and semi-circles twirl around the mother, who is also seeing devilish sights now. A wild idea suddenly inflames her imagination: It's the end of the world, she thinks, *Oy vey*! God, have pity on me!

She runs ahead, the snowflakes lashing cruelly at her face, the capricious storm tossing her every which way. Suddenly, she sees the frightful poles and beams of the barbed wire fence in front of her. She draws back in fright, but through the snowy fog she hears the sentry's deep voice that augurs only ill: "*Was machen Sie heir so spat?*"[19] She shakes with fear. "*Was…*" the voice repeats, awaiting her answer. She wants to flee, but the iron voice stops her. "*Stehen bleiben!*"[20] She stands still, paralyzed with fear. The soldier's silhouette draws near the fence. The shining barrel of his gun is pointing at Shura. She begins to tell him, half in Yiddish, half in German, why she had to leave her home, how she had lost her way until she came to the fence. The soldier, she thinks, is probably barbaric. A shot in the head and it'll all be over! A Jew near the fence at that hour can only be a smuggler or an escaping criminal trying to sneak out of the ghetto. But even the cruel war has not smothered every human feeling in this German's heart. A smoldering ember still glows within the barbarism. He

[19] German: "What are you doing here at this late hour?"
[20] German: "Don't move."

70

looks at the Jewish woman, tries to read the truth in her eyes, which no longer express anything but despair. And he believes her. Her passionate pleas move the young German, but he does not want to expose his weakness. "*Eins, zwei, drei, los*!"[21] he yells, and Shura flees into the dark night. A short while later, the hospital sends a furious doctor to her home, who curses and mutters the whole time as he walks behind despairing Shura.

Shura turns the key in the lock that squeals menacingly They go in. "Where's the patient?" the doctor asks, opening his leather bag. Shura goes to the bed and takes her child's hand into her own. He's cold as ice. "Eli," she cries out. "My darling, my treasure, he's dead! Doctor, maybe he just fainted? Save my son," Shula pleads. She wrings her hands in despair. The doctor feels the patient's pulse, and whispers: "Oy vey, he's dead! His heart is no longer beating." His words are like a landslide of rocks that shatter the poor mother's heart. For a moment, she's confused, incapable of taking in the catastrophe. Then she trembles, like a felled tree, collapses onto the bed,   embracing the feet of her dead son. She does not weep. She expresses her pain in a dreadfully agonizing grunt. Outside the storm rages frenziedly, darkening the bleak scene even more.

The doctor closes his bag, and gazes at the sorrowful woman. Perhaps he is asking himself whether he is needed any more, if he should try to heal the raw wound of the sobbing mother. In the end he decides to say nothing more, for fear of only making matters worse. The pain is too fresh to be soothed, the doctor thinks, and without a word he goes out of the room, leaving the mother alone

[21] German: "One, two, three, get out of here!"

with her son's corpse.

Fifteen minutes later, the mother is still lying on her son's bed. Ideas, determined but confused, torment her thoughts. When the bitter reality finally strikes her a sharp blow, she rises from the bed and begins to scream like a madwoman. Only the groans of the storm answer her from outside.

The days that she spent with her living son now seem to her to have been wondrously peaceful. She hurls insults and curses at God, as if she were taking pleasure in her invective that grows more abusive with every passing minute. Then she calms down, allows herself to be swept up by gloomy thoughts, and suddenly begins twitching. She pulls out her hair with her fists, enjoying the pain. She brutally tears at her face with her fingernails, staring at the blood that streams down her cheeks and hands. The hours stretch out slowly. One minute, they are rent by her mad screams, and the next, they are tempered by the atmosphere of death that turns her body to stone. Very slowly, the light of dawn filters through the frosty window panes, lighting up the tragic scene of a mother grieving the death of her son.

A Mother's Terrible Crime

As Shura looks at Eli's frozen face, a comforting, redeeming thought flashes through her mind. It's not really Eli lying there on the bed, but only a cold, empty body, a repulsive corpse. Why not exploit it to keep her other child, her sick daughter, alive?

Lately, Benitza's appetite has greatly improved, and she's even devoured her dead brother's ration. It seems to Shura that her face has filled out a bit. Small spots of color have spread over her cheeks that her mother hopes are signs of recovery. All thanks to Eli's daily ration, the wretched mother thinks, torn between joy and bitterness. Then she goes over to the corpse to ask its forgiveness: "No, I'm not sinning, my little treasure!" she murmurs, bending over the lifeless body. "After all, you want your mother to stay alive! You want her to respect your memory! Forgive me!" A heavy silence is the only reply.

The worst nights are those when the wind roars outside the window arousing Shura's fear of divine retribution. The storm seems to be threatening her with horrible vengeance, as if God were speaking from the mouth of the wind. "Hang your head in shame, an unfit mother! Hoo, hoo!" the wind roars as it blows through the desert of the ghetto, giving poor Shura no rest until the pale dawn rises...

It never occurs to the anguished mother that she ought to take steps to bury the body of her beloved son, to call for the death wagon, to remove the body from the house, to part from him forever. All of this causes Shura immense sorrow, destroys her. But she knows that tears are foolish and futile. She has already unburdened her pain in her unrelenting screams. And in any case, as long as she lives, she will always carry little Eli's memory in her heart.

Her survival instinct has driven away the oppressive, enormous pain. Shura refuses to die, despite the horrible conditions and the loneliness that are her lot in life. The hunger for life is overwhelming. She examines her reflection in the large mirror, set in a silver frame, and it shocks her. Her expressionless eyes, encircled by bluish-black rings, stare back at her. Her soft, heavy lips lend her face the look of a tormented saint. Her aquiline nose protrudes from her face as if it were not a part of it. Her exhaustion has made new wrinkles appear on her rough skin. Her most recent torments have mercilessly left their mark on her face. Her almost numb legs can hardly bear the weight of her thin body. Nonetheless, despite the dreadful loss of her beloved son, Shura is filled with a mad desire to go on living. She looks at the small, petrified face of the dead boy and a strange notion goes through her mind again and again: why shouldn't I leave the body here and go on getting his daily ration?

But very soon the body begins to stink. Startled, Shura sees it begin to decompose. The stench is so strong that it permeates the entire building, from the ground floor to the attic. The tenants cover their noses when they leave their apartments. "Dear God! What a stink there is here!" They call out, troubled. One even adds – and it turns out, he's right too – "it smells like a dead body!" That man, an undertaker by profession, can tell the difference between that smell and thousands of others. And since the stench is particularly strong outside the Beigelmans' door, he decides to go himself to question Shura. He knocks on the door. To be on the safe side, Shura hastens to cover the body with a blanket, and then, with a pounding heart, she walks towards the door, calling out: "Sorry, I'm very sick. I won't open the door; I'm afraid there might be a draft." "I'm not asking you to open the door. Just tell me where the awful smell is coming from. It's filling the whole building," the angry neighbor calls out from behind the door. "Oh, yes... it's from my place. I had some poison against worms and I left it in the basket too long. And now it's rotting," Shura replies, shaking like a leaf. "What are you waiting for? Why don't you throw it away? How can you live with such a stench?" "I'm sick, I couldn't get rid of that garbage. But now that I must, I won't put it off any longer." "Then get a move on, so we won't have to talk about it any more," the neighbor calls out instead of bidding her goodbye, and walks quickly down the stairs.

When she no longer hears his footsteps, Shura touches her feverish temples with her frozen fingertips. *Oy vey*, she moans in desperation. What now? Shame, disaster, humiliation! Those are the piercing words that come to her lips. Only now does she realize what a crime she has been guilty of. She is shocked and her whole body shakes. You are the one who has committed this crime! What a shame! You are neglecting the body of your son instead of burying him with respect so he can rest in peace, an inner voice cries out to her. And Shura says to herself, it's probably the spirit of my son seeking revenge. It must be God intervening on Eli's behalf. With a sense of revulsion, she looks at her face in the mirror, the face of a living-dead woman. At least I can save my little girl, the last treasure left to me in this world, she thinks. To save her from death, I must go on living and do something. Trembling, she moves close to Benitza's bed and bends over to kiss her blue lips and her sunken cheeks. Her gaze meets the child's clear eyes and they seem to be pleading with her. Benitza's emaciated hands point to Eli's motionless body, and a despairing groan escapes her throat. A stream of tears suddenly flows from Shura's eyes onto the girl's face. Cry, Mama, Eli's dead, the child thinks, and she too bursts into tears. Shura sits down heavily on the edge of the bed, and with a bleak expression, thinks about what she should do. She presses her fists to her feverish temples, but all of her efforts to concentrate are to no avail. Her thoughts sweep her far from reality. When she tries to think, she is assailed by horrifying spectacles and hair-raising sights. I don't care, she says to herself, I will leave the body here and exploit the situation as much as I can.

But when Shura conceived of this gruesome plan, she had not expected the body to give off such a terrible stench. An awful thought suddenly enters the mother's mind, and does not loosen its grip. How can you make such calculations, when your son's body lies here in front of you? God, dear God, but all this is for my little girl, the only thing I have left, the life I still hope to save.

Benitza's Death

Shura motions towards the immobile ghostlike figure. But the ghost does not move, remains indifferent, gazing with dimmed eyes at the emptiness. "Shura, Shura," a deep voice resonates. "What do you want from me, Yoszek, my husband?" "You ask me what I want? What I want? You've already killed one of my children, and now you are planning to kill the second." "I didn't kill him, and I am sacrificing my life for my daughter," Shura insists in a pitiful voice. "Be still! Take your child and run away. Death is already stalking you." The skeleton takes several steps, his eye sockets fastened on pale Benitza. Shura screams. Yoszek disappears. The hands of death have tightened around the child's scrawny body. Shura tears her daughter from the cold vise-like grip and tries to flee. But death has an iron fist. The poor mother pulls with all her might, while the frightening skeleton continues to jeer at her.

After a fierce struggle, the exhausted mother releases her grip. Death snatches up the frozen body and vanishes into the abysses of its kingdom.

These nightmares cannot help but leave a deep imprint on Shura's soul. Like the mentally ill, the miserable woman cannot distinguish between reality and the world of her dreams, which she interprets as black predictions.

The little girl's health grows worse. As for Shura, she is helpless in the face of the blows that fate strikes at her from every side.

You must do something! Her conscience cries out, but how can she do anything when all the roads are blocked? Shura resorts to desperate measures to save the light of her life, flickering in her daughter's body. Since she never reported her son's death to the registrar of births and deaths in the ghetto, she still receives his food and bread ration. She maintains her distance from all her acquaintances. Like a thief, she casts worried looks all around, and sometimes covers her head with a kerchief so no one will recognize her.

One day, when she is leaving the co-op, she meets a friend who asks how Eli is. She replies curtly, in a trembling voice, that his condition is stable. The door of the Beigelmans' apartment is closed to friends because Shura is afraid her secret will be found out…

Dear God, dear God! What's the point of taking risks if I am doomed to lose her? What's the point of sacrificing my health for her sake? What's the point of neglecting what's left of Eli's body? Everything is falling apart! How can I bring a doctor here? Oh, God, everything will be found out. Unless I share my dreadful secret with the doctor. The situation is absurd, idiotic - incomprehensible.

Shura feels she is in a bottomless pit. She cannot wrest herself free from the tormenting vice that is gripping her. If she's all alone in the world, she won't let death rob her of the little she has. She struggles for the sake of Benitza. She's already lost one child, she'll fight for the second one like a soldier at the front. Like a lioness for its cub, she says obstinately again and again. She knows she is fighting against an invisible enemy, frozen death that mocks her inhuman suffering.

During the night, her dead husband re-appears in her dream, and in a loud, resonating voice, he calls: "Shura! Shura! Save your only daughter. Death is stalking her, don't you see?" And he points to the thin, blurred silhouette that sticks up like a large statue in the heavy darkness.

"*Avek!*[22]" Shura yells, in desperation…

One day, when Shura is busy disinfecting the room, in an effort to drive out the stench of decaying flesh, Benitza motions to her to come closer. Shura, surprised, goes over to her daughter's bed. Benitza fastens her blue eyes on her mother's face, opens her shirt and shows her where her heart is. She wants to explain something, but only meaningless sounds come out of her mouth. Her poor mother places her hand on her daughter's heart, that mysterious machine that gives life, but she is unable to decipher Benitza's message.

The smell coming from the corpse is causing the sick child great discomfort. Her attacks of coughing, which cruelly exhaust her young body, torment her. Her face looks almost exactly the same as her dead brother's. Only rarely does Shura leave the apartment, but when she has to leave Benitza alone, she goes mad with worry, because she knows how frightened the child is. Without knowing exactly why, Benitza is afraid of the silent body. When her mother returns, the child's breathing becomes regular, calmer. Her eyes, which were widened with fright, return to their natural size, and her bluish lips curl into a smile of pain…

When the door closes behind Shura's back, Benitza's heart begins to leap inside her chest. The loneliness terrifies her. The gloomy silence heightens her anxiety. The storm roaring at a distance fills her with dread. How bad she feels without her mother! How lonely it is in the room! How sweet her mother's heavy moans are to her ears, even the curses and threats she hurls at the directors of the ghetto!

[22] Yiddish: "Go away!"

Only the presence of her beloved mother can bring a love-filled smile to the sick child's lips. From her corner, she looks distractedly at the dust-covered furniture. But suddenly she notices the frozen face of Eli lying in his bed.

He's sick, the child thinks with dread, Eli's sick, very sick. Mama's gone to call a doctor to treat Eli, my dear brother. I mustn't wake him. Her gaze moves again over the room. She mutters: Eli's sick, I mustn't wake him, he's asleep.

Indeed, he is sleeping, an eternal sleep, far from the hardships and suffering of the ghetto...

Night has covered the ghetto with ribbons of mourning. It has spread its black mask over the accursed life of the ghetto's inhabitants. Sleep, land of lepers, until dawn comes, the source of new torments, Shura says to herself. But woe to Shura, sleep is not a synonym for forgetting. Her dead husband, wrapped in white, haunts her nights, and hurls at her – such horror! – curses from beyond the grave. The dim eyes of the dead man stare at his wife, who draws away with frightened steps. In a roaring voice, he asks: Where is my son, Shura? Where is he? Tense with fear, she shows him the silent body lying on the bed.

The dead man's cloak, like the storm, whirls in a dance taken from Hell:

> Woe, to a mother whose humanity is lost
> What a catastrophe and shame you've caused
> Eli, your beloved son, you have not buried yet
> Oh, what a punishment you will get
> For your terrible crime!

"Dance! Dance! Atone for your sin, you evil woman! May you know no rest," the husband shouts. "Benitza is dying too. Save your daughter, heartless mother!"

"Mama, save my sister," Eli's spirit pleads.

Shura wrings her hands, "I don't want to live!" she cries out in a heart-wrenching voice.

"You must go on living," her dead husband replies in a dull voice.

"For what? For whom? How?"

"For your only daughter! For this treasure, this soul that has never sinned," Yoszek's spirit speaks, in a whirling, melodious voice.

"*Avek! Avek!*" the dead man thunders, and with a gesture of disdain, he commands her to let him pass.

She squeezes into a corner of the room. The indistinct shadow of the ghost bends over Eli's body. "Get up!" the voice from another world calls out, and Eli rises as if he were alive. "Dance, dance!" the voice roars, so loud that Shura's blood runs cold. The two dead figures, the father and the son, begin to turn and twist in strange, coordinated movements, to the beat of a quiet melody of blackest oblivion. They move their arms and legs, drawing closer to terrified Shura. Then they grab hold of her arms and push her into the middle of the room…

God is avenging me for my terrible crime, Shura thinks. A stupid mother, that's what I am. It's not worthwhile sacrificing yourself for your child. That's not so, it is worthwhile, and Eli's spirit is happy to sacrifice his body for such a lofty purpose. As Shura struggles with herself, she is torn between contradictory emotions. One day she feels her action is justified, the next day she thinks just the opposite. This inner struggle drains her of all her strength, and exhausted, she collapses onto Benitza's bed…

The cruel fate, Benitza's death, actually takes place on a pleasant day. Shura, overburdened by her endless troubles, lies on the edge of her daughter's bed, immersed in her thoughts.

Suddenly Benitza's body shakes, her face grows pale, her eyes open wide and her lips move in a strange tremor. "Benitza, Benitza," Shura screams wildly, clasping the emaciated body with trembling arms and murmuring, "Benitza, my sweet one, my baby, what is happening to you? I'll run to get the doctor, hold on." The child's eyes, filled with love, hang on to her mother, and a smile appears on her lips. The flame of her life is going out in her mother's pleasant arms. Benitza returns her soul to the Creator. "*Gevald! Gevald!*[23]" the piteous woman screams, tearing clumps of hair from her head. "*Mein kind, mein kind,* you're dead! I don't want to believe it!"

She collapses onto her dead daughter's bed, and kisses the small white face. And so she spends the whole night. The dawn, like a terrible nightmare, creeps into the dark room…

A ghost is suddenly standing in the middle of the room, and in a bleak voice recites a poem:

> Towards death, towards death
> We walk, we march
> What is our life, in the face of death
> The death we know not and do not want to know

After uttering this bitter truth, the ghost vanishes into the mysterious darkness, and instead of bidding her farewell, he hisses at Shura: "Listen to the voice of your heart and your conscience!" The music fades into the distance, and Shura's soul is lost in the emptiness. Two days later, she awakens covered in sweat, and her gaze falls on

[23] Yiddish: "Woe is me!"

the body lying serenely on the bed. The cruel reality, ten times worse than the bad dream, shoots like an arrow into her lost consciousness...

The room is small and its ceiling is low. Stars flicker through the small window. In the middle of the room, stand a table and chair. Shura, sunk in her thoughts, sits on the chair. A Jewish woman with black, shining eyes and hair as black as a raven. Her hands support her chin, and her gaze is fastened to one spot. Finally she moves her lips, a slight movement that is hardly discernible: how immense my disaster is! How desperate my condition! If God had only left me one of my dear ones, a ray of light to illuminate my hellish life! But the Creator has left me no one. All three have been taken from me. Only despair and loneliness are left to me. Why hasn't he taken me too into the kingdom of heaven, so that I may rest with my children? He has punished me severely. There are people who thirst for life as a man thirsts for water. Perhaps I too am such a person. I don't have the courage to end this filth called life. Shura, defeated, loosens her long hair and passes her fingers through the black mass. For a while she remains standing in one place, and finally, with a dull moan, falls back on to the chair. I don't know what to choose, she mutters, tormenting life or cold death.

Choose death, a voice from another world thunders from afar. Slowly a skeleton cloaked in black enters the picture. Shura stands erect, and with a mechanical movement, bends her head back and with indescribable dread, looks at approaching death. Have you come to take me too? I don't want you! Go away! Far from my eyes! What will I do now, wretched woman that I am? Shall I go on suffering? I no longer have anyone in the world, and no desire to live. I am torn between life and death. I must decide between the two. Shura reaches out her hands, and in a deathlike voice she says: There in the Marysin cemetery, stand the mute tombstones of people dear to me. At night, the storm laments and the accursed souls cry out. By day I visit my dead loved ones. In the silence of death I can weep on their graves and speak to them. What will happen to me? I turn towards life to help me, but I know that is impossible. Life shows me a direction covered in blackness, a path that moves towards the infinite. Only death is left to me. Who knows you, mysterious ghost? Who moans with your roars of pleasure?…

Shura's Trial

Shmul Kinder, the undertaker, a neighbor of the Beigelmans, is no fool. From the first, he realized what trick Shura was playing. Although he did have some doubts, they were soon dispelled once he obtained proof. I've got to exploit the situation, the traitor said to himself, and a cunning smile spread over his lips. This desperate man, whose only thought was how to save his own skin, was also suffering from hunger. And now, a golden opportunity had presented itself, and Shmul Kinder was determined not to let it get away. This little, skinny Jew was preparing the ground for the Beigelman family's loss. He informed the recorder of births and deaths and the police, and then with a light heart and a head full of dreams, he is preparing to build his happiness on the ruins of his neighbors' life, and to fill his starving belly. He expects to get a generous reward from the Jewish authorities, and perhaps – who knows? – from President Rumkowski himself!

Everything proceeds according to his devilish plan.

The police break into the Beigelman apartment. Stunned by the horrible scene in front of their eyes, one worthy of Dante's Inferno, they do not dare touch the prostrate woman, who is passionately kissing a dead body.

"Why don't you say anything?" One of the policemen shouts at Shura. "We came here to carry out our duty, all the rest is no concern of ours. Arrest this criminal woman and let that be an end to the whole affair!"

The mad woman is immediately placed in a dark, dank cell in the infamous prison on Zsernitzki St. She sits on a plain wooden plank chewing her fingernails until she draws blood. *"Mein kind,"* she murmurs tenderly, and at once bursts into laughter. "Yoszek! Yoszek! Come see me, come dance with me." After these fits of madness, she withdraws into an endless state of shock.

And here Shura's tragic story comes to an end.

In the Lodz ghetto thousands of such tragedies have taken place, some far worse than Shura's. Is it possible to describe hell on a sheet of paper? Not even the greatest writer in the world is capable of doing so.

Anyone who has crossed this horrific swamp in his lifetime will never forget it...

The day comes when Shura, broken and defeated, must stand trial in the ghetto's court. The best seats are taken by the privileged residents, who hunger for scandal. These honorable gentlemen want to watch a play, and Shura is going to star in it. The trial looks promising; it'll be a great spectacle. Everyone waits expectantly for the proceedings to begin. The honorable gentlemen are probably waiting to see a cruel mother who tried to save her own life at the expense of her son's corpse. Nonetheless, some think she had other motives for behaving the way she did. But most of those present agree that she deserves to be accused of selfishness and deviant behavior. Finally the trembling Shura is led into the courtroom. Hundreds of curious, pitiless eyes try to see into her soul.

The trial is conducted according to the accepted procedures. Yes, no, Shura replies, and she doesn't seem to be present in the courtroom. "Woman," the judge asks, "do you admit to the charges?" "To the act, yes, to the crime, no," Shura replies in a quiet voice, accompanied by a deep sigh. "Don't you think it was a selfish act, to leave your son's body in order to fulfill your own needs?" the judge asks in an intimidating voice. Shura is about to answer, but instead of speaking she bursts into ugly laughter, which soon turns into a confused mixture of meaningless words.

The spectators sit up straight, stunned. It's as clear as daylight that the accused woman has gone mad. The judge looks around the courtroom and then announces in a loud voice: "The trial is cancelled for obvious reasons. We have not succeeded in clarifying this issue, and it seems we never will." He bends forward, leaves his bench, and signals to the crowd to disperse. The courtroom slowly empties.

Cruel mother! A mother who has lost her humanity! What have you done? Hang your head in shame!

Afterword

Now that I've finished writing my story, I'd like to place before my readers a problem of conscience that has been troubling me: Can we call this woman a cruel mother? Is she really heartless, has she no conscience? Her love for her son is indescribably immense. Then why, after his death, did she defile his body to supply her own needs? Was the real motive in this affair really egotism? Can this woman's thirst for life be likened to self-love?

I ask my readers to trust their own reason, to delve into Shura's soul and to judge her actions themselves.

The Veronsky Family or
The Trials and Tribulations of a Young Poet

"Master Henrik, drink a cup of tea!" Marisia calls out in a sharp voice. But to no avail. "I'm warning you. If you don't drink it, I'll take it back to the kitchen." Silence. The maid places the tray on the floor and peeks through the keyhole. Then, her hands on her hips, she straightens up and mutters: "I knew he was writing another one of his crazy poems. Damn the man who invented poetry. May he burn in hell forever!"

Marisia did not know that Pegasus, the source of poetic inspiration, had left this world ages and ages ago. The only thing she knew was that her young master, Henrik, was suffering from a slight case of madness, and that this weird peculiarity of his was the cause of endless quarrels in the family.

"So, Master Henrik, are you going to let me in or not?" "Stop pestering me with your tea. Spill it out the window and that'll be the end of it!" Henrik replied, irritation showing in his voice.

"Dear Jesus!" Marisia whined, "and to think that I brewed this tea especially for you, and took the trouble to bring it to you!"

"If so, then take the trouble to return it to the kitchen, because I'm very busy right now."

Despite this clear rebuke by her master, Marisia did not go away, because it was the lady of the house herself who had instructed her to bring Henrik tea.

Suddenly the door leading to the main salon opened, and Henrik's mother entered. Her face, lightly powdered and rouged, wore a very severe expression. Her makeup did not hide the wrinkles on her face, a sign of approaching old age. She wore a long black dress that trailed on the floor like the tail of a faithful dog. She had thin lips and a cold, authoritative gaze that made simple people uncomfortable. She was very sure of herself, like most aristocrats, and walked proudly across the salon. From her haughty bearing, it was obvious that she took pleasure in her authority. She was worried about her only son who, in her opinion, had strayed from the straight and narrow path.

"What trouble has my son caused you this time?" she asked the maid, who usually began trembling as soon as she saw her mistress.

"Madam, if you only knew! I brought the young master tea, and he rudely sent me away!"

For a minute, the lady of the house gave Marisia a piercing look, and then, in a soft but firm voice, she said: "Go back to the kitchen. I'm going to demand an explanation from him."

And in an instant her well-manicured hand was resting on the gold-plated handle of the door to Henrik's room. Henrik, seated at the mahogany desk in his quiet room, was engrossed in writing a poem that was slowly but surely taking shape. Again someone was knocking on his door! The maid's persistence was infuriating the boy, and he angrily shouted: "Stop bothering me! I don't want and don't need any tea!" "Henrik, I insist that you open the door and stay calm, do you understand?" Mother! Henrik thought, and calmed down at once. He opened the door. Marie – that was his mother's name – glanced quickly at the desk covered with papers and notebooks. Her eyes flashing with anger, she walked deliberately towards the sofa. Sitting down, she crossed her legs. A soft light, whose rays filtered through a bluish lampshade, lit up her flaring nostrils and the stern expression on her face.

Her mourning dress nicely complimented her slim figure and emphasized the serious demeanor of the aristocratic woman. Gold earrings glittered on her pinkish ears. Henrik sat on a chair in front of his mother, obstinately saying nothing. "Listen," she broke the silence. "What do you mean by speaking rudely to Marisia? Where are your manners? What will happen to you, my son? Your father and I planned to make a rich and important man of you so that you would not shame our family, but you, such a crazy boy, are devoting yourself to awful, unseemly activities, that take up all of your time and are totally useless." "Mother, how can you say such things? Art and poetry enrich the soul, raise man above the mediocrity of life, but you, because you lack imagination, allow yourself to adopt such a negative attitude." He straightened up in his velvet-upholstered chair, and excitedly tossed his mane of curly black hair. "I refuse to become a money machine. I spit on that filth called money that drives the passion of greed. I have other plans, other dreams." "No," his mother dryly interrupted him, "You will be what your father was, and since he wasn't a poet, you will not be one either." "No, I will decide what I will be and what I will do. In the meantime, I want you to leave me in peace. I want to devote myself to my work and I want that idiot Marisia to stop nagging me." "You insolent boy! Your audacity knows no limits. I will discuss this with your father, who will deal with you severely. What you have just said is nonsense, a youthful caprice that will pass when you grow up."

Marie got up, cast a cold gaze at the desk, and quickly

left the room, her earrings shining brightly and the train of her dress fluttering lightly. A silver comb held her large bun of hair in place. Her silhouette vanished behind the door, and the boy remained alone with his morose thoughts. His mind was filled with rebellion against parental authority.

What does that mean, that I cannot be what I am? Must I give in to an external influence? Must I follow a path I have not chosen for myself, but that my parents have dictated? Never! I will never give up my plans, I will never tarnish my soul. Shame! Disgrace!" But then a contradictory voice scolded inside him: "How can you oppose parents who want to see you take the right path? What will your father say? How will he judge this affair? With uncompromising determination, with authority and rigidity!"

Henrik was apprehensive about a talk with his father, whom he knew all too well. His father had always regarded poetry as foolishness, a source of useless error. He depicted it in derisive terms – wandering in the clouds, the work of Satan, a dangerous flaw.. This attitude of his was causing Henrik suffering. He had even tried to oppose his father, but had failed miserably. Only deep in his heart did he cherish a belief that no one could challenge. He tried to drive away all these ideas that so oppressed him, and returned to his work.

Henrik bit the tip of his pencil, in an effort to channel all of his creative forces into his poetry. But to his despair, a landslide of thoughts descended upon him, and he no longer felt the full force of divine inspiration. Far from it. The words refused to flow. At the high point of his creation, when the young man and woman, embracing one another, were supposed to ascend into the clouds, the rhymes and poetic beauty were totally disrupted.

Incapable of completing his poem, he put down his pen in despair, dropped into an armchair and tormented, fell asleep. In his dream, he saw his father grabbing him around his waist and his mother's face redden with anger, and he himself wrestling out of his father's grip, falling into a fathomless darkness.

The Classroom

"Hooray! Math," cheers a diligent student, with a simian face that glows with glee as he looks at Henrik. But Henrik hates that subject with all his heart. In his opinion, it is a cruel monster, a science bereft of fantasy that clutches the mind in the claws of narrow, dry logic. But the cheerful boy with the monkey face strides over to the blackboard, and draws a heavy chalk line under the menacing word: "Mathematics."

Henrik gnashes his teeth. He would gladly choke that human caricature. But at once he is alarmed by the criminal thought that has passed through his mind. In the meantime, the young genius, like a skillful acrobat, has begun to amuse himself with numbers and fractions, arousing Henrik's admiration. Ah! Dear God! If only I could do such things! Why am I so different from him? He asks himself. Suddenly, a mysterious voice asks him: Henrik, would you really like to be like him? Does his mundane character suit you? No, definitely not, the boy answers firmly, but at the same time he keeps looking at the young mathematician who is explaining the tricky formulas to his classmates who are having a hard time understanding them. Henrik recalls that he too found them difficult and that he had failed to solve the problem. Who should he turn to? To him? Certainly not! But how will he get out of the quandary? If he doesn't solve the equation, his face will be covered with shame, in front of all of his classmates. I think I'll ask him a favor, anyway, he thinks, he won't be able to refuse me. He gets out of his seat and goes over to the star of the class, who gives him a mischievous look, as if he's about to ask him something.

"Please, Spotanski, explain this hard problem to me too," Henrik mutters. "Hard, hah, hah! It's as easy as pie!" Then Spotanski grabs his notebook, and with the speed of lightning, begins to cram all of his knowledge into poor Henrik's brain. "Enough, enough," Henrik pleads with his teacher-classmate not to get carried away. Spotanski starts over again, this time with exaggerated slowness, but soon goes back to his usual galloping speed. Henrik groans, swearing he'll never ask Spotanski for help again. The classmates standing around them all burst into laughter, confirming the rightness of his decision. "It's not my fault that you're so dumb," Spotanski says. This insult is a hard blow to Henrik, but knowing that his classmate's knowledge is far superior to his own, he is careful not to retaliate with a slur.

Spotanski looks with amazement at Henrik, who, with a defeated expression, goes back to his seat, sunk in gloomy thought. What a strange fellow! The young genius blurts out, and carries on with his mathematical juggling.

Suddenly Professor Koneiski comes into the room. A short, spectacled man, filled with vitality, he is possessed of perfect logic. Placing his umbrella in a corner of the room, he cries out, "Dear God, what a downpour!" The pupils can hardly restrain their laughter. Drenched, Koneiski looks as if he's just come out of the shower. But what is even funnier are the drops dripping onto his crooked nose from time to time.

The professor removes a textbook from his briefcase, and immediately becomes engrossed in it, a look of amazement on his face. In fact, Koneski is a mathematical genius. He rifles through several pages, and raises his eyebrows as if he's asking: "Children, where were we?" The pupils all respond with confused, loud answers. "Please don't shout," the professor calls out, banging his fist on the desk and knocking the inkwell into the air. "Spotanski, can you remind us what we were studying in our last lesson?" Spotanski stands up and replies without hesitating. "Show us," the teacher says nodding his head at Spotanski, who goes over to the board and begins solving the mathematical problem again. He gaily draws a line under the solution, and throws the class a kiss. "Return to your seat. Your solution is excellent!" the teacher says with satisfaction, as he looks at his favorite pupil over the rim of his glasses. Spotanski bows and goes back to his seat.

"Henrik Vronski, to the blackboard!" The boy was so lost in his thoughts that the pupil in the seat next to him has to arouse him with a blow of his elbow. When he recovers his senses, he gets up, walks to the board, still somewhat distracted, his eyes glued to the blackboard. The professor dictates a new problem, leaving poor Henrik confused. He looks from the chalk to the blackboard and from the blackboard to the chalk, but his head is empty. "Idiot," the best student in the class calls out, breaking the silence. Henrik's face reddens with anger and shame. He still says nothing, waiting for the teacher to release him from his torment. The verses of the last poem he had written ring through his mind. Now they seem very strange and pathetic. In his imagination he now sees his mother, who so much wants her son to become a man, not a parasite. A youthful caprice that will pass with time, his mother's voice echoes in his head, the voice that had so hurt him. Start doing something useful and profitable! His mother vanishes, to be replaced by his father, who frowns dourly, as he always does whenever he's in a foul mood and says: I want a serious explanation from you.

Professor Koneiski, who is losing his patience, cuts Henrik's reveries short: "Well, are you able to solve it or not?" "No," Henrik mutters. "Go back to your seat, you're an incorrigible jackass!" The word "jackass" strikes Henrik like a lightning bolt. He's unable to move, and in despair, clutches the chalk in his fingers. A question perturbs him: Why? But he understands it's an absurd question. "He knows math, and I don't, so I deserve to be called a jackass," that's the explanation he gives himself, and deeply troubled, goes back to his seat. He grabs his head with his two hands, unable to stop thinking about himself. Am I really a jackass? Is that mechanical caricature worth more than me? Why, for heaven's sake? Other than mathematics, that jackass doesn't know anything. In any case, I won't be mocked! I won't allow others to look down at me! I won't allow it! It's out of the question. No, I won't!

Large tears fall from his eyes onto his math notebook. The loud bell announces the end of the lesson. Professor Koneiski leaves the classroom but comes back immediately to get his umbrella, which is still soaked.

Spotanski, surrounded by a circle of friends, is jeering at Henrik. "The Professor asks him if he knows the material, and he stands there like an electricity pole. No other pupil would have waited for the professor to expose his ignorance. That's why he's a jackass," the outstanding pupil adds and continues sending supercilious looks at Henrik, who is sunk in thought. Henrik suddenly feels as if his body is on fire. Without hesitating for a minute, he gets up and stands in front of the top pupil in the class. Until now everyone has seen Henrik as a nice and inoffensive friend.

But their opinion is about to change completely.

"Shut up!" Henrik roars. "A human caricature without dignity or conscience!" he adds in a still but firm voice, and walks away. Spontanski had not expected that kind of reaction. What a volcanic outburst! A chill runs down his back, and he resolves never to make fun of his classmate again. But this painful experience has already shaken Vronski to the depths of his soul.

How nice our street is, Henrik thinks as he returns home from school. At the end of the lane, beneath the blue sky, he can see the contours of the Vronski family mansion, a red brick building surrounded by lush greenery.

The boy goes into the entrance hall and climbs the staircase. The sound of his steps is muffled by the carpet that covers the stairs. His parents, as usual, are waiting for their son to join them at the dining table for their family lunch.

A Family Meal

Henrik goes into the dining room, takes his seat next to his father and waits for the maid to serve the first course. Only a minute goes by before smiling Marisia comes in, all out of breath, carrying a tray of steaming cabbage soup in ornate porcelain bowls. She is surprised to see that Mr. Vronski is not his usual jocular self, but one glance at his dour face tells her he is troubled. The soup is served in an oppressive silence. It must be because of our young master again, Marisia says to herself.

Not wanting to annoy anyone, the maid forgoes her usual chitchat with the family and goes back into the kitchen.

All three eat in silence. Although Henrik has a huge appetite and the soup is excellent, he hardly manages to swallow any of it, and from time to time he steals glances at his parents, wondering at their strange behavior. A quarter of an hour goes by. Helena, a tall blonde girl, brings in the other courses. Every time Helena serves them, Henrik glances quickly from the corner of his eyes at her face and breasts, fearful that his expression may be giving away his lewd thoughts. Helena has a hook nose, a grudging smile, and constantly wears a serious expression on her face. She has recently been hired to serve in the Vronski household.

When she removes Henrik's plate, her hot breath and the scent of her perfume caress him. His face reddens, and to make matters worse, she remains standing next to him. A shameful thought leads him down the path to temptation. To think that she's so young and has such a nice figure, and I can't embrace her! Get out of here! Away with you, temptress! He sends these pleas from his heart towards Helena, who is now nailing him to the cross by asking an unexpected question: "Why are you so red? Do you have a fever?" Mr. Vronski turns his eyes toward his son. He understands everything, Henrik thinks sadly, and prays to God to make him vanish immediately. After putting the tray down, Helena places her hand on Henrik's forehead, and it seems to him that he sees a scheming flash of cunning glittering in the girl's eyes. If his parents hadn't been there, Helena would certainly have fallen into his net. Instead of calming the patient, the hand resting on his forehead only heightens the scarlet spots on his cheeks.

Worst of all is Helena's buxom chest right there under his eyes. "Nothing serious, a bit of fever, that's all," she says softly, and Henrik has the feeling that she would have willingly consummated the sin right there in front of his parents. Then suddenly – what a relief – the temptation, the sin and the girl all leave the dining room at once. Henrik sighs deeply. The strange meal is over. Mr. Vronski lights a cigar and begins to talk to his sinful son: "My friend, consider yourself lucky that I still call you my friend, even though you've turned into an enemy." "But, Father!" "Keep quiet!" Mr. Vronski roars and puts down his cigar, which is sending smoke rings towards the ceiling. "It's time to think about your situation, you foolish boy! You've invested all of your thoughts and time in shallow poetry, and nothing else interests you any more. If it were only a hobby, I wouldn't object. Everyone has the right to devote some time to frivolous pursuits that do no harm. But you are gaining satisfaction from this nonsense, and that's where the problem lies. You are neglecting your stud-ies, you aren't spending time with your friends. A real monk! What's happening to you?" Henrik, his head bent, remains obstinately silent. "I demand that you change your behavior, a minimum of obedience, do you hear me?" the father rages, and he beats his fist down hard on the table, sending the glasses up into the air. "Yes." "I do not want to hear about these reveries of yours up in the clouds, and not about…those poems." "No, Father," Henrik mutters, his face white as snow. "Yes!" the father cries, rising from his chair, infuriated by his son's obstinacy. His mother sends Henrik an authoritative piercing look that makes it clear he ought not to show any resistance. "If you don't change your behavior," the father threatens, "all of your poems will go up in fire." "What?" Henrik shouted, "Father, you wouldn't do such a thing." "Yes, I will, do you hear me? You have pushed me to the limits of my patience, and if necessary, I will do that too." "A father has no right to do such a thing," the audacious boy blurts out, rising from his seat. "I have no right? What did you say, you insolent boy? Out! Get out of my house! Go!" Now the father also rises from his chair, and pointing with his finger orders Henrik to leave the dining room.

With a heavy heart, in a rebellious mood and a confused mind, Henrik leaves the room. He slowly walks down the stairs sunk in gloomy thoughts. Helena stops him on one of the stairs: "Why are you so sad?" she asks. He gazes into the servant's blue eyes, and although he does his utmost to act like a man, he blushes to the roots of his hair. "Leave me alone," he replies and continues on his way. Helena remains standing on the stairs, stunned. I'm a sissy, that's all, Henrik says to himself bitterly. The slightest thing can make me turn red like a girl. I quarreled with my father and I couldn't even defend myself as I should have.

Spotanski may be right when he calls me a jackass. Oh, God, dear God! A cascade of tears begins to flow from his eyes. But with an effort, he manages to control himself, remembering that he's a man and that tears won't help in any case.

The Escape

He wandered around the streets, his mind empty of all thought. He looked with admiration at the beautifully arranged store windows, observed the mechanical movements of a policeman, gazed idly at a match floating in a canal, and was sorry when it disappeared into the sewage.

Groups of rowdy, laughing hooligans drew near. Henrik envied them their tattered pants made of coarse cloth, their peaked caps, their habit of spitting through their teeth, their rough speech. He even envied the obscenities they hurled at one another. He would have liked to dress like them, to get rid of his fine clothes and join their gang.

As if they'd have me! He thought. They're sharp. They'd only have to take one look at my face and they'd know who I am. They'd manage to get my watch away from me and my fountain pen, but first of all, my money. I'm not one of them, even if I could dress and talk like them. My face and my movements tell them that I'm an aristocrat.

Henrik watched them until they were swallowed up by the crowd and disappeared. A devilish idea popped into his head. He was so hungry for freedom that he was prepared to pay a high price for it by doing something he knew was wrong. I'll go talk to Franek Michalowski, the wildest kid in the class. I don't care what happens! I'll be like him, despite my parents' disapproval. He'll lead me to the mysterious, dark world. At long last, I'll be a man.

Henrik stopped in front of the dark entrance to a shabby wooden house that gave off a bitter smell of poverty. At a first floor window, the freckled face of a girl with a braid appeared. She was gently watering small onion plants. When she caught sight of Henrik, she stuck her tongue out and began staring curiously at the strange clothes the young man was wearing. Henrik drew closer to the window and asked her where Michalowski lived. "Here, do you want something?" she replied in a thin voice. He hesitated, and then, prompted by temptation, went into the entryway. He continued into the room, looked it over shyly, and said in a low voice: "Hello. I see your brother's not here, too bad!" "He went to buy bread, he'll be back soon. You can wait for him," she said. Henrik sat on a chair, but it collapsed under his weight, so he soon found himself on the floor. "Ha, ha, ha" the freckle-faced girl burst into laughter. "You sat on the broken chair, ha, ha, ha!"

Just then Franek Michalowski came into the room, astonished to find Henrik there. Am I crazy, or what? He thought. I wonder why he came to visit me. "Hello, Michalowski," Henrik said, ill at ease, and extended his hand to his classmate. Franek responded by reaching out his coarse, slightly deformed hand. "Vronski, you, here? Did someone send you to me or did you want to ask me for something?" he mumbled. "No, you see, I don't want anything from you, I just came to visit." "You came to visit my poverty, my broken furniture? It's no fun here, my friend." "Not everyone can be rich," Henrik replied. "But that's no reason why there should be so many poor people," Franek said bitterly. "You sat down on a chair that was falling apart, hmm, and got a real blow to your ass, huh?" he joked. From under his armpit, he drew out a loaf of black bread and placed it on the table. "Marishna, pass me the knife, so I can eat a chunk of this bread!" The girl, humming a cheerful song, handed her brother a long, sharp knife. After spitting deftly and spouting a few juicy curses, Michalowski stuck the knife into the loaf of bread. "Mouse, mouse, be quick on your feet, before the glutton comes to eat!" he sang to himself while cutting the bread. He then devoured a huge piece, hungrily and very noisily. Marishna hugged her brother and ate some bread greedily too. "Listen, you want to come with me? No point in staying in this shack with some poor old woman. Let's go have ourselves a good time!" Franek suggested to Henrik.

Henrik looked into his friend's coarse, freckled face. His hook nose and the devil-may-care expression on his face made him look like a hooligan. Pimples and blackheads marred his skin. In the street, the lamps gave off a dim light. Franek took a coin out of his pocket and blew on it to bring himself luck. Deftly, he threw it into the air, and caught it again, just as skillfully. "How clever you are!" Henrik cried out in amazement. "Take the damn coin and do the same as I did." Henrik took the coin and tossed it up high, but it fell on the sidewalk with a loud ring. "What a no-good fellow you are," Michalowski called to him, "Go ahead, try again!" Henrik, red in the face, threw the coin again. This time he had a howling success. "Bravo!" his pal congratulated him. One more time, Henrik said to himself, to work up his courage, and threw the coin again. But he unintentionally let it slip through his fingertips, and the coin rolled quickly into the gutter. "Idiot!" Franek raged, his face red with fury, "Where am I going to get money now?" "Don't worry, I'll give you four times as much," Henrik said boastfully. "You've got that much? Good for you!" And the two shook hands in friendship. Henrik grimaced with pain, and pulled his hand away from Franek's grip. "I hurt you, oh hell!" "No, Franek, you're a good fellow!" "We're almost there," his friend said, and sticking two fingers under his tongue he emitted a loud whistle that momentarily struck Henrik deaf. Similar whistles replied like an echo. The two went past the entrances of gray, crumbling buildings, passing by some low shacks. Franek treated each of the street lamps to a spray of spit. When he missed, he went back and tried again until he hit the target. Finally, they stopped in front of a tall building. A gang of rowdy boys had set up their headquarters there. They played boisterously, spitting, cursing, and laughing. When Henrik and Franek drew near, they welcomed them with coarse jokes and obscenities. "Who's this guy?" a red-headed boy in rags whose breath smelled of alcohol called out. "Put your hands down!" Franek roared, "or I'll break your teeth." The redhead understood at once and kept his distance. "Michalowski!" called out a tall boy who answered to the endearing nickname Watzek-Longlegs, "Are you playing?" "Give him some money for starts," Franek told his friend. Henrik took a large coin out of his purse and handed it to Michalowski. "Would you look at that? You've got piles of money, huh? Why didn't you tell me? Come closer and play with us." Then to the others, "This is a classmate of mine, Henrik Vronski." "A good head on his shoulders, huh?" "Whose turn is it now?" The gang looked Henrik over from head to toe. "Hey, Franek, with his velvet suit, your friend looks like a real prince!" Adek the redhead called out, unable to take his eyes off the new boy. "I bet he's got a pile of money in his purse," he whispered in a sarcastic tone. "I'd gladly smash his face in for him!" Franek threw the coins at the wall. One of them flipped over, and after turning in a large circle, fell right next to another coin. With his hand, he quickly measured the distance between the two. "Swell! This is my lucky day! Did you see that?" Franek said, as he went down on his knees to pick up the money he had won, and stuck it into his deep pocket. Now it was Henrik's turn to throw his coins, while standing on a line that had been drawn on the ground earlier. His coins scattered close to the wall. Then it was the turn of Adek the redhead, and with a roguish grin on his lips, he won Henrik's coins. The game grew wilder, and when it became really heated, Adek the redhead kicked Watzek-Longlegs, who he suspected of cheating. Then Watzek punched Adek hard in the jaw, making a cracking sound. Blood flowed from the redhead's face, and he grabbed the long-legged boy by the lapel of his jacket. The two stood, glaring at one another. "Let me go!" Watzek hissed between his teeth. "Nothing doing," Adek groaned. Longlegs, infuriated, punched the other boy hard in the ribs. The redhead came back with a strong blow to Adek's chin that left him trembling. A cat climbed on the fence, Franek hummed another cheerful tune, and together with the others drew closer to the two adversaries…He encouraged them, egging one on and then the other. "Smash his face in," a hunchback, whose nickname was Little Pony, called out in a sharp voice. "Let him have it! Now's the time!" yelled Antus the Thug. "He's finished!" Franek commented, when he saw that Watzek was losing the fight. Adek, his eye puffed up, covered with grime and mud, tripped Longlegs, who collapsed. "Mt. Everest has toppled!" Franek shouted, and spat in the face of the hunchback, who had come too close to the cluster of fighting boys. The hunchback wiped the spit off his face, and began cursing and whining.

Henrik kept his distance, unable to see any part of the fight because of the tight circle of spectators around the battling boys. He managed nonetheless to see the end of the fight: the redhead, seated on Watzek-Longlegs' stomach, was brutally avenging the dirty trick his rival had played on him. Infuriated, Henrik pushed his way in, separated the two wrestling boys, shoved the vindictive Adek off and released his poor victim, whose face was covered with blood, bluish bruises and mud. But Franek stopped him with a kick to his butt. "Damn it, don't stick your nose into something that's none of your business," the redhead yelled in a menacing voice. Michalowski lifted a stone and threw it deftly, hitting his target. The redhead let loose a few vulgar curses, but Franek hurled another stone, and the redhead scurried away like a rabbit. "If I catch that son of a bitch, I'll break him in two!" the bruised Watzek cried. Then Henrik took leave of Michalowski and began walking towards his house. Engrossed in dismal thoughts, he heard his friend's repeated whistles growing dimmer as he walked further away.

The Return of the Son

A man was walking alone in the street, and Henrik asked him the time. A quarter to midnight, the man replied. Henrik's head was spinning, and he was terrified. I just can't understand it! How could I have stayed out so late? Dear God, what will Father and Mother say? Ah, what a miserable sinner I am! What will happen to me now? Thinking these thoughts, he began walking faster. The leaves of the trees were shaking in the wind, as if they were excited. The strong fragrance of roses intoxicated the boy. The full moon peeked out from between the clouds and flooded the quiet lane with a silver glow. The further Henrik walked from the outskirts of the city, the more the landscape changed, becoming a beautiful park. The sweet scent of flowers surrounded him. He smelled them with pleasure, momentarily forgetting the scene that was awaiting him at home. He finally stepped into the familiar lane, his heart pounding.

Dear God, what will happen now? But a minute later, he resolved to oppose his father's strict authority.

Slowly the outlines of the Vronski house emerged against the background of the greenery. The moon cast a silver light on half his body, while a soft shadow obscured the other half.

On the terrace, Henrik encountered Jan, the Vronski's faithful servant for the past fifteen years. "Dear Jesus, where did you disappear to, young master?" the gentle man asked, scrutinizing Henrik. "Your parents have been to the police, and they've begun searching for you. Madam was almost sick with worry. All the servants are on the alert.

How could you disappear for such a long time?" Jan asked in a soft voice. Suddenly Marisia appeared on the terrace, and when she noticed Henrik she hurried back to the entrance and loudly announced to everyone in the house: "Henrik's here! Henrik's back!" All the servants sighed with relief.

Mrs. Vronski was sitting on the couch in her son's room. Her husband sat alongside her, a dour expression on his face, puffing nervously on his cigar. When she heard the news of her son's return, the mother naturally wanted to run down and bitterly admonish him, but her husband held her back and ordered her to sit down again. "I do not want to quarrel with him now, let him spend the night with the servants. But tomorrow, when he reports to us on his shameful behavior, he had better be careful," the father said dryly and walked out of the room. In the dining room, he encountered his pale son, stammering and mumbling in an attempt to explain. "Stay away from me, you ingrate of a son!" the father roared. "In the meantime, you can sleep downstairs, it doesn't matter where, as long as you are not near us! We will talk tomorrow!" The father left his finger hanging in the air, pointing towards the door, until Henrik left the room.

Henrik walked heavily down the stairs, despondent and miserable. He opened the first door he passed, and found himself in a small, dark room. He would not have been able to see a thing in the total darkness had it not been for the light of the moon. In the corner, on a cot, someone was sleeping restlessly, muttering feverishly. Henrik drew closer, and saw a sweet familiar face. Helena! He thought and wanted to leave quietly, but the floorboards squeaked, and Helena awakened and sat up on her bed. "Who's that?" "Shhh, don't be afraid, it's me Henrik." "Henrik, she repeated the name, surprised. Did you want something?" Suddenly, Henrik felt stupid. First, because he had awakened Helena, and second, because he didn't know what to say. "Listen, Helena, I had a quarrel with my parents and wanted to spend the night with Jan, but I went into the wrong room." "God, why should you go to sleep with Jan?" "Because that's the punishment I've been given." "I see!" she began to laugh. Now Henrik could see her clearly in the moonlight. Her blonde hair was disheveled, her eyes were wide open and her chest was rising and falling rapidly. A wave of heat swept over him. Such a wonderful opportunity! He was alarmed by his own thoughts. You're going to sin again, this time an unforgivable sin. Run away quickly, get away from this satanic, dangerous woman! But despite the danger, he could hardly restrain his inner glee. "Come closer, Henrik. Don't go to Jan. He snores terribly. There's an empty cot near the window. It's made up and clean," Helena suggested. Henrik's eyes closed involuntarily and he felt as if he were going to fall asleep standing up. He groped his way over to the other cot, and lay down. But after a quarter of an hour, he began tossing and turning impatiently. "What's the matter, master? Aren't you comfortable?" Helena asked. "Damn, this mattress is so hard!" he muttered. The servant put on a robe, got out of her bed, and holding a pillow, went over to Henrik. "Get up, master, I'll try to arrange the bed so it will be more comfortable." He did as she said, and very soon he found himself under a down comforter, his head lying on a pillow. "Thank you," he whispered. "I think you may have a fever," Helena said, and put her hand on Henrik's forehead. I don't believe it, that girl is always checking my temperature! Henrik thought, amused. "Yes, I think I do," he said, very pleased without knowing why. Helena's maternal concern annoyed him, that wasn't what he wanted from her. "You're treating me as if I were a baby," he complained. "Ha, ha, ha!" Helena burst out laughing, and then pretending she had stumbled, she fell on to his bed. Henrik caressed her golden hair, and the devoted mother turned into a passionate tigress. Her blue eyes shot ardent glances at him. Henrik embraced her hungrily, and everything around him began to swirl. He felt Helena's red, tempting mouth clinging to him. He felt as if he were going mad. As he kissed her open, fleshy lips, the thought that he was about to commit a sin went through his mind, but it was soon wiped away by his frenzied passion. Her young, slim body drew closer and closer, and Henrik felt an inner fire devouring him. Fiery, wild kisses, unrestrained! Becoming one! Eternity!

When he woke up, Helena was gone. He was covered with sweat. What have I done? He thought. He could see the picture of his sin before his eyes, plain as day. Where is she? That temptress! Ah, yes, she's gone to work. And where am I? In the depths of hell, the voice of truth answered him. And yet, just a moment ago, I was in heaven. "Keep away, keep away, Satan is pursuing me! Yes, I am a heartless son, a conscienceless profligate, who has no place on the sacred earth!" He had the feeling that the sweetness he had snatched from Helena's lips was becoming a bitter poison. His head was heavy. A dull, troublesome pain was pressing on him like a rock. He saw his sins and their awful implications in the clearest light. The ghostly figure of his father, whose terrible anger was making him frightfully anxious, gave him no rest. God,

God, forgive me, he murmured ardently. The door opened, and Jan, gloomy and thoughtful, came into the room. As usual, he was immaculately dressed, the silver buttons of his servant's uniform shone and his polished shoes glittered like a mirror. But now his face looked different. He stood there frozen to the spot. A shadow had now come into his calm life, a life of service to the Vronski family, confusing him. When he had first entered service with the Vronskis, everything had gone smoothly. And devoted Jan liked it that way. But as Henrik had grown, several small disagreements had piled up and turned into the source of loud quarrels. Despite Henrik's tendency to be frivolous, Jan felt a great affection for his young master. His own son had died of a terrible disease, and his wife had died giving birth to him. Jan had remained alone in the world. He was fortunate to have found a position with the Vronskis, where he had always been an extremely devoted servant, becoming the favorite of the household.

Jan had never neglected his duties, which to him were the most important thing in his life. He was constantly bowing, like an automaton, and always had a pleasant smile on his lips. He knew several foreign languages fluently, and when guests came to the house he served them with style. That was the word Mr. Vronski used when he was in a good mood. Jan would speak to the guests in French, mixed with several words in German and a sprinkling of Polish. What an educated servant! The guests would remark admiringly to Mrs. Vronski, who would glow with pride. Tall, elegant Jan always responded to these compliments with endless bows. But his impressive manners were only an outer shell. In fact, Jan was a retiring, thoughtful man, whose circumstances in life had led him to become a servant. Henrik and the other servants were the only ones who knew the real Jan, while Henrik's parents knew him only superficially.

It was very distressing for Jan when he had to tell the boy that his father wanted to speak to him. Knowing his master's fiery temper, the servant expected a tremendous flare-up. Henrik, his whole body trembling, got out of bed and dressed quietly. Standing at a distance, Jan saw how upset the boy was and he went over to him, placed his hand on his shoulder and gazed warmly into his eyes. "Listen, my boy," he said after sighing deeply, "don't aggravate your father. Try to soften him up by behaving submissively." "I'll try," Henrik whispered mechanically, trying to hide his tears. His head dropped heavily on Jan's chest. "Don't cry, my son," Jan comforted him, gently caressing his disheveled locks. "You have a bright mind, you are a poet, and you want to be free, to go your own way. Your parents are blocking your ardor. I understand all too well what's happening." Henrik began to sob, despairing even more now that he felt his desires were as fatal as a toxin. Jan thinks I'm a moral person, but he's wrong. I'm corrupt, I've chosen the wrong path. My parents wanted to save me, but it's too late now. And as he thought these thoughts, his distress soared. "Listen, my boy, calm down now," Jan said, "anyone as sensitive as you tends to suffer, but when you suffer, don't show it. Don't give away your feelings by crying. On the contrary, hide your suffering deep inside your heart. That's the only way you can become a man. Now, my little one, you're still a child." Those words, so full of understanding, shamed Henrik and made him feel unworthy. He pulled himself together, and after combing his hair carefully, prepared for the fateful meeting. He shyly knocked at the door. A silence punctuated only by his heartbeats. Then the resonating sound of his father's voice: "Come in!" Henrik found himself facing a parental court. Instead of lowering his head, as a pupil would do when caught in a mischievous act, he held it proudly high. Father and son engaged in a duel of intense looks. The father's gaze became more and more stern, and more and more expressive, while the son's gaze remained unchanged.

Mr. Vronski expected his son to show submission, to apologize, but the son remained obstinately silent refusing to allow his parents to see into the depths of his defiled soul. The atmosphere was unsettled, suffocating and unpleasant.

The father broke the silence in a sarcastic tone: "I thought the young master would ask forgiveness with the proper degree of humility, but it seems he owes no one any explanations…For the hundredth time I am telling you, you have disappointed us." "That is true," Mrs. Vronski concurred. "For the last time we are addressing you as your parents," his father continued, "because in another minute we will turn into merciless judges." Henrik said nothing. A turbulent storm of thoughts and feelings was raging inside him. He wanted to shout: What do you want from me? In any case, I'll stay what I am! But he could clearly see that such words would only make things worse. "You are being rebellious and disobedient," the father went on in a severe tone, "and last night you snuck into the house like a robber or a drunkard." Henrik's gaze fell on to his desk, which was now empty of all his notebooks. Only a few books were piled on it here and there. He felt a sense of foreboding. He interrupted his father with a loud cry: "Where are my notebooks?" "Burned in the fire," his mother replied, proud of her husband's act, whose duty it was to bring their son back to the straight and narrow path. "Yes," Mr. Vronski stated wryly without a trace of compassion. "We have taken this extreme step so that you will finally realize that poetry is a destructive pastime as far as you are concerned!" Henrik began to shake. Something had broken inside him. "My poems!" he cried out in desperation, and it seemed to him that that same fire had consumed a part of his soul. "My God, the child has gone mad!" his mother called out, running towards her son. "No, Mother, you're wrong, I haven't gone mad. Who gave you permission to burn my notebooks? Do you know you have destroyed your son?" The mother looked at him, stunned. "Keep your distance from this wreck of a boy, Marie. He's acting out a tragedy for us, a wonderful actor, that's what he is!" Mr. Vronski roared. "I'll never forget what you have done! You'll be accursed!" The son cried out in a sorely aggrieved voice. "Out! Get out of my house! Go back to the street, you revolting boy! You have no place in our family," the father banished his son. The mother collapsed on the couch, muffling her sobs. "I have no need of your tears. They only wound and infuriate me even more. You did not know how to respect my sensitivity. Instead you mock it, you hypocrites! I'm not your son anymore!" Henrik bawled, but before he could finish his sentence, his father slapped him hard. Reddened with anger, Henrik raised his fists in a threatening gesture towards his father. "How have I sinned to God that I deserve a son like this?" Mr. Vronski muttered. Marie's sobs grew louder. Suddenly Henrik felt pity for his mother, but the feeling passed quickly, overcome by his fury when he recalled her treachery. "A curse on your heads!" he bellowed as his farewell. Like a young predator, he strode through the dining room, oblivious to everything around him, and disappeared outside the door. On the staircase he met all the servants who had gathered there. Hostile looks and muffled whispers: "The poor Vronskis, their son is such a disappointment!" Marisia said after Henrik passed her. "What a good-for-nothing!" muttered Katya the servant, a peasant girl from a remote village. On his way, good-hearted Jan stopped him, and advised him to leave the house at once. "It's not appropriate for you to remain here," he said. "Your rebelliousness has not surprised me. Your parents have done you much wrong. Go my son, go! You will suffer much in your life." Henrik took leave of Jan and went out into the street.

The overcast sky darkened. Blasts of wind recalled the roars of rapacious dragons. Slowly the clouds covered the windows of light in the sky. The wind ordered the dust in the street to go forth in a diabolical dance. The trees murmured meekly as the storm shook their rustling branches. Loud peals of thunder roared gloomily. Dreadful flashes of lightning rent the canopy of the heavens. A downpour began to fall. Henrik, his head empty, wandered through the streets, and a terrible thought pounded in his mind: I am a criminal.

Chanetzka's Tribulations

Chanetzka is a skinny ten-year-old girl, with a gentle, pleasant face and permanently sad eyes. Her black hair is always standing on end, and a thread of snot is always dripping from her pretty nose. But why is Chanetza worried all the time? Why don't her eyes ever show a glimmer of joy?

Here is the reason. Life tortures her as if she were a grown-up. Cruel tuberculosis has taken her parents from her. The girl wandered around the streets of the ghetto until her aunt took her in. It would be more correct to say that her aunt was forced to adopt her. Willingly or not, she had to obey the orders of the ghetto authorities, upon which she heaped endless curses. And we should understand her because the authorities could have put the child in the care of any of the "notables" among the ghetto's residents, rather than place her with her aunt, a poor, simple woman who is starving too and has no interest in her niece's problems. In short, the aunt took in the child, added the child's ration to her own, and together they boil their soup in one pot. But the wretched orphan isn't happy under her aunt's protective wings. Often she sends her to the stores and the cooperatives, and of course, Chanetzka cannot "go wild" and buy everything she'd like. At an age when everyone sees things in rosy colors, she is sunk in the ugliness of life, which spares her none of its worries or humiliations. It is no wonder that her eyes are sad and her face is serious. In the loud, rowdy lines at the shops, she has picked up some bad habits and vulgar words. As if through a mist, the child sees what was and no longer is –

the years of her golden childhood, her mother's soft, gentle hands that pampered her with love. Brokenhearted, she groans when she remembers her beloved parents, her little sun-splashed room, full of toys that sweetened her carefree life. All that was before the war, but now it is all gone, Chanetzka says to herself. She knows that the war is cruel and terrible, because she herself has experienced its hardships. She also knows there is a front and there are battles, not just far away but here too, close by, in the unruly lines that people stand in to get their crumbs of food. How many times has this child witnessed scenes of bestiality, how many times was she herself the victim of punches to her skinny little body? But this violence is nothing compared to the mental anguish that torments her. Isn't she often called a scrawny mouse and sometimes a walking corpse? This last insult is very widespread in the ghetto. Anyone called by that nickname is fated to die a merciless death. Chanetzka sits on a stool near the window, and through the pane she looks at the sad passersby, at policemen, at the officeholders, and on the other side of the street, behind the large windows, she looks at the seamstresses sitting at their black, dismal sewing machines. Tak-tak-tak, the needles clack. The women's bent shoulders and the pale faces of the young apprentices look at her through the windows of the sewing shop. The skilled hands of the workers glide over the fabric of the shiny dresses under the clamp. And the phut-phut-phut, that enormous noise made by the machines turns into one word – o-u-t-p-u-t! We are slaves, that's what the working women, with their bent backs and dreary looks, seem to be saying.

Chanetzka is used to seeing children walking to work

early in the morning, half-asleep, hungry and beaten. She herself is an apprentice in one of the sewing shops, but she is lucky to work only in the afternoon.

In any case, the air in the morning is just as cold, biting and insufferable as that in the afternoon. Chanetzka has learned to face the ordeals of her fate without complaining or crying. Her favorite pastime is to sit near the window and look through those parts of it that are not covered by frost, at life in the street. From time to time, a wagon loaded with sacks of flour passes by with men harnessed to it instead of horses. It seems to Chanetzka that these men have a horsy look and even behave like horses. All they are missing is a tail, she thinks sadly, and in her imagination, she draws them, gently and with humor, as they would look with a horse's tail. Sometimes, a sewage wagon goes by, with horsemen harnessed to it too, giving off an awful stench. The carriage of the king of the ghetto passes by there only rarely; Chanetzka actually managed to see it once. Then she had her nose glued to the window pane, devouring the President with her gaze. His head was white, majestic, exuding grandeur, and from the height of his seat he looked down at the poverty of the ghetto. Here is the man who with a wave of his hand can send thousands to their death. Here he is, the man whom all the Jews fear like the plague, and who also curse him among themselves, Chanetzka thinks. And with a feeling of respect, she recalls the sovereign's impressive head.

"Chanetzka!" she suddenly hears a voice call her. The door opens and her aunt comes in, as yellow as wax. "They're handing out salami," she says in a screechy voice, and Chanetza tenses up like a coiled spring. She knows she has to take the ration coupons and money, and go stand in line, outside, in the terrible cold. It's so pleasant at home; the fire in the middle of the room is humming gaily. A picture taken before the war shows her aunt smiling pleasantly at the little girl. No sign of bitterness or greed! Life in the ghetto has turned her pleasant aunt into a real, almost satanic wild animal. Chanetzka does not even know what to call this monstrous woman, a bony woman with gnarled fingers and a sour face.

Chanetzka goes out into the frozen, windswept street, wrapped in an old, torn coat. Brrrr! Her face grows blue, her nose turns red, and she cannot stop the tears from running down her cheeks. The line is very quiet. Confused, she stands motionless. What is going on here? No one is quarreling, no one is cursing, no one is kicking, no one pushing. Strange, very strange. Leaning against a white wall of snow, she begins to stamp her numb feet on the frozen pavement. One after the other, the people blow on their fingers, stamp the ground with their feet, swaying grotesquely. "Damn it, when will they let us in already?" asks a young man who has lost his patience standing in the bitter cold. "Porter!" the people yell, "Let us in. It's icy out here, we're starving, and we're freezing!" Silence. "He couldn't care less that we're freezing," a woman moans. Another shouts, "Egoist!" And yet another, "Heartless!" Curses come raining down on the head of the hapless porter, whose feet are also quickly turning into blocks of ice. Finally, the long-awaited moment arrives. The line suddenly comes to life. A tin can flies through the air, and a woman screams: "You're choking me! Help!" Someone falls down on to the snow, and his ration cards drop from his hand. A tall man, wearing a bizarre hat, smashes his elbow into Chanetza's stomach, and a street-child crushes her tiny toes with his wooden clogs. "Oh, God!" the poor girl whines, as a hand suddenly pushes her out of the line on to the pavement. Confused, she stands there holding her ration coupons. At once, all those in line are swallowed up into the store, and Chanetza is left sobbing bitterly. "Why are you crying?" the porter standing at the door to the store asks her gently. Chanetza raises her head, astonished by the sound of a humane voice. "I...I...was standing in line and they pushed me..." she stammers, bursting into tears again. "You poor little thing! I had a little girl just like you, but she died. She looked so much like you. Enough! Enough, don't cry. You'll get in without standing in line." A faint smile lights up Chanetza's face. She wipes away her tears, and goes inside.

She hands her coupons to the supervisor, pays the cashier and takes her ration of salami, after it has been weighed precisely down to the last ounce.

She goes out into the street, and the porter bids her goodbye with a warm smile. "Nu, my child, aren't you even going to thank me?" Chanetza's turns her blue eyes to the man, opens her mouth, but is unable to get a word out. "All right, go then!" the gatekeeper mutters, gesturing with his hand, "Look at that, the children of the ghetto! They've got no manners!" "It's really unfortunate," a "respectable" intellectual woman agrees.

Aunt Manya – that's the name of Chanetza's guardian – goes to work early in the morning and leaves the little girl at home. Chanetza watches with disgust as her aunt prepares her breakfast. She picks up the breadcrumbs in her crooked, trembling fingers and sniffs them. She greedily licks a drop of oil that dripped on to the table.

Before she goes out, she assigns the little girl a long list of grueling tasks: Remember, there may be meat today! Go take a look to see what's going on in the cooperative. Maybe there's still a coupon for parsley left in the vegetable ration book. Don't forget! Don't forget!" And she leaves without so much as a parting word. When she's left alone, the child feels a sense of relief, of freedom. Behind the windows of the sewing shop across the street, the work has been going on at a fast pace since the morning. Today something is different. The windows aren't totally covered by frost. One of them, strangely enough is clear, still transparent, while the others are hidden behind a thick layer of frost. So the child can happily watch the seamstresses at their work.

She often looks at a picture of her aunt taken before the war. A pleasant, round face, full cheeks – Manya and her triangular chin display a broad smile. But suddenly, right in front of the girl's eyes, the yellow, starving monster appears, in such sharp contrast to her former appearance. As she always does, Chanetza sits on a stool watching the agile movements of the seamstresses. Sometimes she runs from the window, embracing the stove with her hands, enjoying the warm vapors it gives off. Just a week ago, she had the appetite of a wolf, but lately she has lost all desire to eat. She hardly manages to swallow her soup. On the other hand, she would be happy to eat a slice of bread, but where could she find one? The hours pass with monotonous slowness, the days stretch out, life goes on. On the table, the clock performs its regular, dull task, ticking indifferently, moving its hands forward with the passage of time. Chanetza has the impression that it trembles, gets bored, and cries, shouts...Stupid life! Vain life! Tick, tick, tock... The child has the feeling that the clock is ticking out the word "Co-op" followed by her aunt's words "Don't forget, don't forget! Go see what's happening there!" Tick, tock, tick tock. In front of her eyes, a warm bun rises and falls straight into her hands. Her white teeth are about to bite into the soft dough. In fact, the bun is hard, it's impossible to take a bite of it. "Give it to me!" Aunt Manya yells in a malicious voice as she draws near the child. "No!" the child screams. Her aunt's nose grows longer, her eyes grow large, and her fingers begin to move, to bend, and to wave in the air as if in a spectral vision. Chanetza runs away, clasping the bun to her heart. The witch chases after the orphan, her cold fingers encircling the child's neck. Ice, dread, a look of madness. The child lets go of the bun that rolls away and vanishes together with the nightmare. She opens her eyes, rubs them, and suddenly hears the monstrous voice of her aunt. Don't forget! Go see what's going on in the co-op, maybe there's parsley there…

Panicking, she puts on her coat, grabs the ration coupons and the money, and rushes out in a frenzy. Breathing hard, she bumps into a young man and asks him: "Is there any parsley?" His only reply is a yawn. "Is there any parsley?" the child yells in his ear. "I'm not deaf! No, it's finished." "Dear God," the girl mutters. "And do you know if there's any meat?" she goes on. "There was," the young man replies indifferently. "And what's left?" she asks in a pitiful voice. "You little idiot, stop pestering people with your questions! There was meat, but now the store is closed. *Laden iz fardig!*"[24]

She runs off, her head full of gloomy thoughts: I've got nothing to bring home. My aunt will beat me… When she

[24] Yiddish: "The store is closed."

129

gets to the dreary entrance to her building, she sees her aunt's ominous silhouette, mercilessly cursing her. "You filthy little bitch! You're letting me die out here from the cold? You went out without leaving a key with the neighbors! Do you think this house belongs to you? What do you think you are, the owner of the house?" her aunt screams in a vicious voice. Suddenly she tears the key out of Chanetza's hand, turns it in the keyhole, and opens the door. They go inside.

"I heard there was meat today, and parsley and celery. It was a great day! I hope you went shopping," Aunt Manya says. "No," the little girl says, as pale as chalk. "What no?" her aunt screeches, as if someone had poured boiling water on her. "Wh-h-y?" "Because..because…I was dozing," Chanetza replies, starting to shake all over. "What do you mean, dozing?" "I was sitting on the stool and I fell asleep." "You lazy piece of work! Such a shiftless dreamer. ! Now, because of you, I'll have to fast, to suffer!" She stamps her feet and spits in all directions. It takes nearly half an hour before she calms down.

Chanetzka walks to the sewing workshop, exhausted, her heart pounding with fear. Aunt Manya, stretched out on her bed, stares at the ceiling with dull eyes, swallowing her saliva. Then she gets up, tiptoes over to a small tin of sugar that belongs to her niece, because she has already emptied her own tin of sugar. In the wink of an eye, she swallows all of its contents, nearly fainting with pleasure. When the little girl returns from her work, she is unable to taste any food, and only wants to gulp down glasses of water and cups of black coffee. "What's wrong with you?" her aunt asks one day, worried by her niece's small, pale face. "I only feel like drinking." "Drinking? Maybe you have a fever? I feel like eating, and you want to drink! Ha, ha, ha!" she laughed hoarsely. She borrows a thermometer from a neighbor and hands it to Chanetzka. "Take your temperature," she orders her. The child places the thermometer under her armpit, and sits down on the stool. Ten minutes go by. Her aunt takes the thermometer and lifts it to see the numbers in the light filtering through the window. "You've got a fever. That's all we need now! Thirty-nine! Welcome to our home, expenses and worries!" Days pass, but the fever does not go down. The sick little girl convulses from attacks of fever, rolling from side to side like a puppy. Finally, Aunt Manya goes to fetch a doctor, whose diagnosis is severe pneumonia. "Mazal tov," her guardian complains. "She must be given more food," the doctor says. "Doctor, to me of all people, a poor woman who has nothing but Rumkowski's food ration to live on, to me they've entrusted this child! They forced me to take her, because no one wanted her. And now she's sick, and it'll cost me a fortune! I have to pay the doctor bills from my own pocket, because the little one makes no money, she's just an apprentice." "Madam," the doctor said, "I think the best solution is for you to submit a written application to the old man,[25] asking for coupons and a loan from the central fund." "That's right. And in it I'll also describe the horrific situation I live in so the President will know," the aunt says. "Definitely," the doctor agrees. "I've written out a prescription. Call me in a few days. We'll see then how the little girl's lungs are. Good day!"

"Good day!" Aunt Manya replies. She remains standing by the sick girl's bed and asks her a silly question: "Nu,

[25] The ghetto inhabitants' name for President Rumkowski.

how do you feel?" "Better," the orphan murmurs. The truth is that she does not feel better. On the contrary, her situation is worsening. The doctor has just made it very clear that she needs more solid food, which in his opinion was the only medicine that will do her any good.

"What will you do, Manya" a neighbor, Mrs. Spitz, asks her. "What can I do? She's nearly dying, but I can't put her in the hospital. What can I do, that's life!" she groans. "In your place," Mrs. Spitz says, "I'd do it anyway," looking at the patient who is burning up with fever. Aunt Manya does not answer. Chanetzka, lying on her bed, says nothing, occasionally uttering a weak moan, nothing more. Her face grows tinier each day, and her breath is very short. She no longer eats, but looks at food with revulsion. When her aunt asks her how she is, she replies: "Better." She does not know what her illness is, and the drawn-out attacks of fever exhaust her. She is dying, fading away, vanishing quietly, without groaning or complaining, without her mother's protective wings, without her sweet kisses. She dies without gentleness or help, but she is unaware of her death. Even before she knows life, she returns to the earth, forever. She gives her soul back to her Creator, leaving on this earth only her miserable, useless body, which in a short time is taken from the house and buried. Aunt Manya does find the strength to go to the offices of the Burial Society, where she orders a memorial plaque that reads: Chanetzka Gutman, aged ten. Then she goes to her home, makes the bed that the child's body has been lying on, and sits at the table to eat her breakfast.

The alarm clock ticks, the hours pass, and hopeless life stretches endlessly. Chanetzka's death has changed nothing.

Elza or Forbidden Love

They met during the war. He was a tall Jew, with brown hair and eyes that glowed like coal but were sad, almost tearful. She was a blue-eyed blonde, a proud German, daughter to the wealthy Grote family. A Jew and a German, two races that cannot be reconciled, a forbidden love, denounced because of the hatred of Jews that flows in the veins of the stiff-necked, arrogant German people.

Her name was Elza. She led a comfortable life in her parents' home, but it seemed that the outside world was exerting its pull on her. She loved life very much – her society, her comforts and her handsome beaux. Her parents, full of good intentions, did all they could to make their only daughter happy. In the spacious rooms of their grand home, her laughter echoed like the sound of crystal. Gertrude – Elza's mother – was a very fat blonde with a double chin, a typical bourgeois woman particularly fond of cheap knickknacks and glass objects. She walked with a heavy tread, and tended to wheeze. A gold pin, inlaid with diamonds, glittered on her ample chest, and pearl bracelets shone on her wrists. Tiny earrings hung from her earlobes, quivering as they kept pace with her movements.

Elza was as light as a butterfly and as joyous as a bird. Over time everything changed, and her childhood traits altered completely. Her look became pensive, and her eyebrows would often be drawn and gloomy, like small threatening clouds hanging above her aquiline nose.

The Grote family had lived for many years in the city of Breslau. Soon after the German occupation of Poland, for professional reasons, the father Bernard decided to move

133

his wife and daughter to the occupied zones, to the city of Lodz, located in the heart of the industrial area. Elza's father wanted to see his daughter marry Roman Burger, the son of a rich industrialist from Lodz. The fact that both fathers had been close friends almost from childhood only reinforced their desire to have their children marry.

Roman Burger was a handsome, blond man, but dull and ordinary. You only had to talk to him for a quarter of an hour to see that in his soul he was no different than thousands of others. He was a muscular, enterprising young man, but there was something cruel about him. German blood coursed through his veins. In short, a good-looking, wealthy young man, but nothing more. Roman visited the Grote family nearly every day, and had begun visiting his bride-to-be with a newspaper in his hand, and would then read aloud to her the news from the front.

Just think, Elza, "What a blow our soldiers have struck the Poles! They are rushing ahead like bulls," he called out loudly one day, and then sat on the sofa, and became engrossed in reading the news. When he was through, Elza's father patted him on the shoulder and said in a festive tone: "Our Fuhrer is the greatest genius of the twentieth century. He will conquer the whole world. His speeches excite and inspire millions of Germans!" Then he got up, gazed at a picture of the Fuhrer as if he were look-ing at God, and in a loud voice dryly uttered the cry that millions of Germans were repeating in unison: "Heil!"

Roman also got up and yelled "Heil!" In a thin voice, stout Gertrude repeated the refrain after her husband and future son-in-law, and Elza, like a mechanical toy, did the same. Then Bernard bent his impressive head over the radio, and began to turn the knobs with his right hand.

"Zzzz..," the radio hissed, and then scraps of conversation, pieces of music and fragments of plays rapidly flooded the room. On the small display, the names of cities marched, one after another. Suddenly, stop! Elza's father lifted his head, placed a fingertip to his lips, calling for silence. No one in the room said a word. The victory speech of the conqueror blasted like thunder. The words hurtled forth like waves of lava from a volcano, crushing and igniting everything that stood in their way. The words burned, sometimes halting for a moment only to burst forth again with greater force. It was the first time Elza had ever heard one of Hitler's speeches. Everyone around her always pronounced the Fuhrer's name with divine admiration. The grating sound of his fiery speech, the horrible stream of his invective hurled at high-placed Englishmen – all of this verbiage that flowed from his mouth upset her. He presents the political situation like a true prophet! How well he knows how to stir up his people with the fire of his ideas, Elza thought. And yet – isn't it a sin, to cause so much bloodshed because of a hunger for power! Isn't it a sin to sacrifice the lives of thousands of sons in order to conquer the world?

She was alarmed by these thoughts of hers. Roman gently touched her arm. "What are you thinking, my dear? Let us speak frankly, maybe for the first and last time! I am about to go into the army, and I am ready to spill my blood for the sake of the Fatherland. You'll see, the war will be over soon. Our genius of a leader will settle accounts with the English! The Fuhrer's flag will fly over London. The Germans will dominate the entire globe. I'll be back, we'll get married, and live happily. Unless I die on the battlefield and...ah! I don't feel like finishing that sentence, you wouldn't be able to weather such a blow." Elza sat there musing. Would she really grieve over her fiancé's dead body? Suddenly, she was startled by the truth. In her mind's eye she now saw Roman's corpse lying on the battlefield, and she herself, bending over it, looking indifferently at his dead face. A thought passed through her mind: No, I don't love him! Why am I pretending I do? He doesn't suit my character, and I have the impression that he wouldn't be too perturbed by our separation either. He treats me lightly as if I were just a friend, and I behave towards him in the same way. Is that really love? No, it's just an act. A game devoid of feeling, devoid of warmth. She struggles fiercely against these alarming thoughts.

The roaring voice of the Fuhrer, which has grown louder following the raucous cheers of the crowd, cut short her reflections. Hate-filled words blared forth from the radio: "The Jews," the speaker screamed at the top of his voice, "must be liquidated," stressing the German word *austottn*. Chills run down Elza's spine. The loud applause and the shouts of the excited crowd were repeated, becoming more and more intense. "Heil Hitler! Heil!" The radio whistled, shrieked and squeaked as if it was about to explode into a thousand pieces. The speech and the thunderous applause fell silent. The electric lights lit up the salon. From the radio came the harmonious melody of a tango, creating a pleasant atmosphere in the room.

Roman always came to visit Elza in his military uniform. In the green uniform of an officer in Hitler's army, he looked even handsomer, really smart. With chivalrous politeness, he would always remove his shiny new cap and walk over to his fiancée. The two young people always spoke about the same subject. He told her proudly that he was about to go to the front and would perhaps be killed there. He expected her to burst into tears, but she did not. However, since he himself was naturally reserved, he did not find this disturbing.

One rainy morning he arrived at Elza's home, pale as death, and sat down heavily on an armchair opposite his golden-haired fiancée. "What's wrong, dear?" Elza whispered. "In another hour and a half I'll be on my way to the front, with all of my gear, on a fast train. Elza opened her blue eyes wide. Roman, drowning in her gaze, kissed her red lips passionately. But to her it seemed like a cold kiss. Roman warmly shook her father's hand, and took his leave of Gertrude with a light kiss on her hand. "Will you accompany me?" he asked, turning to the whole family. "Of course! Gertrude, Elza, get ready! That's the least we can do. When a young man is prepared to sacrifice himself for an idea or for his people, personal interests are of no importance."

A moment later, Roman's father, who closely resembled his son, entered the room. He was tall, broad-shouldered and fair-haired, with drawn eyebrows, a forehead creased by wrinkles, and a grave expression on his face. He stopped by a small side table, placed a heavy suitcase on it, and sighed deeply.

"*Guten morgen!*"[26] He said as soon as he put the suitcase down, wearily as if he were acting against his will. His strange behavior had an oppressive effect on the atmosphere in the room. Despite his fifty-five years, he had a proud walk. He adored moderation and detested all forms of exaggeration. But now the demon of war was already out of the bottle and had dragged his son into its madness

[26] German: "Good morning."

137

in the ranks of the army. Restraint had given way to suffering, the circumstances had driven off moderation, and the fever of war, like venom, had poisoned this man's blood, heart and mind.

They all left the Grotes' home together to accompany Roman to the train station. The young man parted from each of them, one after the other. He squeezed Elza's hand a little longer than the others, trying in this way to convey his feelings.

Tears fell from the heavens. The bulky engine emitted a morose whistle to let the soldiers know they'd soon be on their way. Their helmets stood out against the cloud-covered, threatening skies. In disarray, they climbed into the railway cars next to the platform, the dingy copper barrels of their rifles protruding above their heads. A few people moved about on the platform, making no noise, but caught up in a kind of strange delirium. Processions of faces, moans, smiles, brief truncated sobs. The iron wheels of the serpent-train were examined one last time, and…it was on its way! The dragon gave a tremendous roar and spewed out a cloud of spark-filled steam. The atmosphere on the platform became more animated. Relatives waved their hands excitedly and called out. A child with golden braids called in a tiny voice: *Mein Vater! Mein Vater!*[27] The face of her father, lit up with a slight smile, appeared at a window of one of the long railway cars. His pale hand made a slow movement, a sign of farewell, and then fell back heavily. A woman, her head covered with a black shawl, holding a red rose in her right hand, ran towards the window that was rapidly moving away and handed it, a sign of her love, to a soldier bent over by his heavy load. A

[27] German: "My father! My father!"

138

quick glance revealed that her blue dress hid a shameful pregnancy.

Roman's father, his eyes filled with tears, kissed his son on the forehead. For the second time, the young man bid farewell to all his relatives, one after the other. Gertrude placed her two hands on Roman's pale temples, looked straight into his eyes and said: "Don't forget my daughter!"

"Never! I'll keep her picture next to my heart."

He moved away, finding it hard to recall how all of this had happened. When he was alone, he tried to reconstruct that picture, which had left such a deep imprint on his heart and mind. Hardly eight days had passed since he had taken the decision. It had been just a week ago that had passed so quickly and would never return.

Despair! What should he do? How would he live now? He was in a wilderness. After the volcanic outburst, he was gripped by a sense of dread. And that paralyzing numbness continued. The memory of that scene, of his still fresh decision, gave him no rest, and struck the young man's heart like a bolt of lightning. In his mind's eye, again and again, he saw that picture, so dear and so bitter at one and the same time...

[Publisher's note: This story was never finished]

SCENES FROM THE GHETTO

The Bleeding Soul of the Litzmannstadt Ghetto

When I lived in the hell of the ghetto and saw the flowing blood of my innocent brethren, I decided to put my testimony in writing. I would have liked to extricate the soul of the accursed ghetto from the frozen jaws of imprisonment, and to reconstruct the cruel existence of the inhabitants of Litzmannstadt who were enslaved, dispossessed and exposed to daily dangers and the shock of helplessness. I would have liked the blood to flow over the page, so that the memory of those merciless years would be passed down to the coming generations.

The inhabitants of Litzmannstadt claim, justifiably, that no one will ever be able to describe the hell they live in. But I will attempt nonetheless to gently lead the reader there, and to introduce him, at least in part, to this world, where tragedy and comedy intermingle. I want to enable him to feel the despair of certain scenes, and at the same time to illuminate my description with the burlesque, shadowy and absurd sides of ghetto life.

But the most important thing I'd like to do is to reawaken, honestly and justly, the bleeding soul of Litzmannstadt.

Yossel, Orphan of the Ghetto

The room, as dark as a grave, is scarcely lit up by the faint light of a night lamp. The pale face of the mother – torn asunder from life and lying, regal and proud on her deathbed, indifferent to everything, even her son's despair - is indistinct in the darkness. The face of her son, sitting by her bedside, is as pale as hers. On a small table, a clock ticks off the minutes resolutely and constantly – tick-tock, tick-tock, like the pounding of a hammer.

Life, our only treasure, has left you forever, Mama! The boy cries out and falls like a stone on to the silent corpse. His eyes express enormous, unbearable pain. He sobs bitterly, nearly mad with grief.

He passes a frightful night next to his mother. And, of course, he sees her in his dream. In it, she too cries with hot tears, and a weak murmur escapes her trembling lips: "Yossel, what will you do on this earth? Tell me!" "Mama, I will carry your sacred memory here, in my heart, as long as I live, so that God will help me."

When he awakens, the dream vanishes. The men from the burial society come to take the body and place it in the black, cruel ground. They wrap it in white shrouds, and after preparing it for life in the world to come, they throw it roughly through the open door of the hearse. "Take pity on the body of my poor mother!" Yossel calls out, desperately extending his hands towards the robots of death. "What's the point of being gentle, she doesn't feel anything anyway!" they smilingly answer. Yossel, who is mad with grief, glares at them, and shouts at them: "You don't understand my despair!" "He seems to be a bit off his head, that one," one of the men whispers to the other, and the lash of their whip is already echoing in the darkness of the night. Like a ghostly vehicle, the wagon slides over the pure snow. Yossel follows it with his eyes, stunned. "Take me too and bury me alive next to my beloved mother!" he yells, too late.

At the corner of the street, a blustering wind is shaking a lamp that squeals with an ominous sound and then falls silent. At a distance, Yossel can still see the black spot growing smaller until it disappears altogether. "Silence, wilderness, madness. Mama, how can it be that you're gone?" he mutters. "My sweet angel, as good as gold, as innocent as a child!" With fists raised skyward, he lifts his eyes to the cloud-covered heavens and curses. Diatribes, invective, curses mingle in his mouth with fragments of prayer, and all suddenly drown in a stream of tears as hot as fire. It seems to Yossel that his fiery sobs could burn a deep wound in his flesh. His love is so strong that neither time nor death can extinguish it. From this day onward, an unforgettable, rankling day, the boy will bear the figure of his dying mother in his memory, and he swears it will be engraved on his heart forever.

Yossel remains alone, alone with his terrible suffering that eats away at his very soul. A black week, filled with grief and uncertainty, draws to an end. By then, Yossel is already apathetic, torpid, in a state of total listlessness. But a few days later, his condition takes a turn for the better. After gathering strength and reconciling himself to the situation, he is reborn.

And Yossel does go on living. First of all, because he wants to live, and second because his strength, although much weakened, is not altogether gone. Slowly he recovers his mental equilibrium. But of course that does not cause him to forget his mother, whose memory is preserved in his heart. He goes back to the normal life of the Litzmannstadt ghetto, dragging himself from the house to the workshop and from there back home. In the evening, he devours his supper – a thin soup he prepares himself – stretches out on his straw mattress and at once sinks into oblivion.

The pale winter dawn tells Yossel that the day has begun. Still sleepy, he throws a glance at the alarm clock, whose piercing ticking torments his soul and body. At six-thirty, making a supreme effort, Yossel leaves the soft paradise of his down blanket. He dresses slowly because the terrible cold freezes his blood and his limbs that are still warm from his sleep. From time to time, he stamps his feet energetically, to keep them from turning into blocks of ice. Outside, diamond-like snowflakes glitter on the walls. Strange arabesques of frost pile up on the windows. Yossel washes with water so cold that it seems worse than the venom of a poisoned arrow. Then he makes himself breakfast from his allotted ration – 250 grams of bread – goes out to the stairs and locks his door with a key.

The staircase, made of wood, trembles under the quick footsteps of the tenants. Shouts echo in Yossel's ears: "Don't forget to buy parsley," a sharp voice calls from above. "Let them all go to hell!" an angry voice yells from below. These oft-repeated concerts are very familiar to Yossel, and he is already sick and tired of hearing them. His eating utensils – a tin bowl with a spoon inside it – are attached to the leather belt at his waist and they ring as he walks – ding, dong, ding! Just like an alarm clock! The knocking sounds grow in number, because now the yellow clogs are knocking on the pavement too, and the noises all intermingle. The building on Pieprzowa Street awakens to the life of the ghetto. The street begins to bustle like an anthill. Policemen's caps glow like butterflies, high boots arrogantly invade the street, and the clogs, big and small, bang vigorously on the pebbled streets. Sometimes the voices whisper; sometimes they grow into an ear-splitting roar, which often turns into loud laughter. Who laughs like that? Yossel asks himself. That's how it is. Someone makes a joke, and everyone bursts into laughter.

Yossel turns to one of the passersby: "Dear God! Help me lift this heavy man!" Unfortunately, he has appealed to a skinny, weak passerby, who can hardly stand on his own two feet. "My boy," he replies, "I already have one foot in the grave…" The poor man drags his large clogs over the pavement and goes on his way. "Wait, wait, I'll help you!" a policeman calls out to Yossel, and together they lift the human wreckage. Shaking and breathing hard, the skeletal man gets up on his swollen feet, wrapped in coarse rags. The policeman gives him a friendly pat on the shoulder, and says "Give regards to my grandma up there!" The wretched man moves away holding on to the walls to stay upright. "Here's one more who'll croak soon," the policeman mutters under his breath, and adds at once in a deep voice: "We'll all end up in the Marysin cemetery, including Rumkowski. He'll be the king of the dead." "I wish he were already dead! I wish they'd hang him on the first pole they come across!" Yossel hisses between his teeth. "Our Socrates is as healthy as an ox!" the policeman says and looks at the boy, and then goes back to directing traffic.

Yossel's gaze is always fixed on the sewing machine, its motor ticking cheerfully. Its hum joins a chorus of other machines. Next to Yossel, a worker is knitting away furiously to catch up on lost time. A sea of heads bent over coal-black machines stretches as far as the eye can see. Most of them are women, young women in particular. They don't stop working for a minute, but at the same time, they laugh, shout, tell all kinds of stories; in short, they try to lighten up the drabness of their lives as slaves. The foreman, a young, elegantly dressed man, marches back and forth on a kind of small corridor between the rows of machines, supervising the working women.

Inside the workshop, Yossel is quieter. He devotes himself, mind and body, to his work. The incessant movement has an intoxicating effect. He breathes deeply, and already feels better. But woe to him, after a few hours at work, hunger and fatigue, like a recurrent nightmare, make his limbs numb. Gloomy ideas now cut off the pleasant feeling that had overtaken him earlier. Fortunately, before too long the sweet voice of the foreman announces the lunch break. Get ready for battle! The pots, the saucepans, the bowls chatter. The working men and women, who together with their machines had formed one inseparable block only minutes before, now all rise quickly from their places.

In the line, Yossel's gaze meets that of a woman laughing nervously. Oh, she's nearly a corpse, he thinks, as he looks at her glowing face, its neatly sculptured lines. The woman's voice pierces his ears. Why is she laughing? She has no reason to be happy. Her laughter is completely artificial. Yossel, assailed by blind rage, is ready to punch the old woman in the face. But he stops himself at the last minute, because he suddenly realizes her gaiety is an affectation. Maybe she is hiding her sorrow behind that laughter? Maybe her pretense at gaiety is helping her forget her sorrow, just as sleep enables me to forget mine? Those are the things Yossel says to himself in a kind of internal monologue. Desperate hunger cuts short his philosophical musing. Terrible pangs torment his stomach, and trying thoughts fill his mind incessantly, drawing him into a terrible delusion: in his imagination he sees a fresh loaf of warm, fragrant bread. And now he sees himself going towards the object of his desire with a knife. But the bread flees, and on its way, passes right under Yossel's nose. Yossel has lost everything; he finds himself standing in front of an emptiness, still holding the big knife in his hand.

In the meantime, our dreamer has stepped on his skinny neighbor's foot. Aye! The victim yells, and begins to hurl dreadful curses at Yossel, who was lost in his daydreams. The man spits straight into Yossel's face. "May your feet swell up like mine! May your eyes come out of their sockets! May you go blind!" he hurls a barrage of curses on our distracted philosopher. "But, I…I..didn't do it on purpose," shamefaced Yossel apologizes. The man calms down and draws his swollen face closer to Yossel. "Look," he whines, "see what my head looks like, like a watermelon." The poor man's eyes are so sunk in his swollen face they can hardly be seen. "Look," he goes on, "my legs are as straight and rigid as poles, my stomach is like a sinner in hell," the starving man says. "I no longer believe in anything. I've lost my father, my mother, my sister and my brother. I'm all alone in the world." Yossel feels a sense of identification with the poor wretch, who, in addition to his physical suffering, is also sunk in despair. So then there are people worse off than me, he thinks with

149

a bitter smile, and then, with a sense of shame, says to himself: Woe to anyone who gloats over another's misfortune. Before we go on with our story, let us introduce the reader to the history of the ghetto's kitchens. At first, in 1941, the kitchens were private. Then they came under the city's control, that is, under the supervision of Chaim Rumkowski.

Even if your countenance was frozen, or completely despairing, Eva, the woman who handed out the food, remained indifferent. She was the queen of the pot, and sometimes a slight movement of the ladle in her hand was enough to sweeten your life. What a miserable life! Yossel thinks as he looks at the thin soup that is supposed to give him enough strength to keep on working. A good soup could really have warmed his heart! It's really awful that I'm not in fat Eva's good graces!

Now it's the turn of the worker with the sad, submissive face. Eva twirls the ladle in every direction, and the pessimistic customer's eyes follow her affected movements with rage. "You're deliberately dropping the potatoes back in," he complains, and his eyes gaze at the young woman, her delicate face and chubby cheeks. "Mister, you're never satisfied with your portion of soup, you're always complaining!" "Maybe you're not as hungry as I am. Give me a few miserable potatoes and I'll be happy and satisfied." "Under Chaim Rumkowski's protective wings, no one can be satisfied! After the war, I'll invite you over, then I won't be stingy with the potatoes. I'll even roast you a goose!" "Talk is cheap!" the sad worker answers angrily. "After the war, I'll be the one to invite you!" "Ha, ha, ha!" Eva bursts out laughing, as the half-starved man, his head bowed, walks away holding his bowl in his hand, stirring angrily with his spoon. Even from a distance, his grumbling can be heard, "I should have gotten two hundred grams of potatoes. I wish her the good luck to stay alive after the war, that one…!" The line moves ahead; some grumble, and yet others are so miserable, they have to be forcibly driven away. There's a hold-up in the line. Those waiting are upset. What's going on? Why aren't they handing out more soup? They've got full stomachs! They don't care a fig about our hunger! Complaints are muttered and shouted aloud. The human snake has stopped advancing because of one of those human shadows that fill the ghetto. The wretched fellow gazes longingly at the pot of soup. Then he winks at Yossel and grumbles: "Water, that's all! It's not enough to fill a hole in your tooth! Dirty thieves! The portions aren't full! It's robbery! Damn it all!" And then he looks distractedly at his empty bowl.

Yossel, after receiving his soup ration, goes back to the sewing machine. He pushes aside a pile of fabric and puts his bowl in its place. He chews each piece of potato with gusto, sniffing it loudly. A worker sitting near him has just finished his meal, and he licks the last drop off his spoon. "Hey," he calls to Yossel, scratching the back of his neck as merchants do, "does the soup have any effect on you?" "The only thing I feel is that the soup is very hot and it burns my guts," Yossel replies, placing his bowl and spoon on the floor. Behind the boy's sewing machine, a group of workers sit, spitefully recalling the delicacies they remember having eaten before the war. "I used to eat at the *À la Fourchette*[28] restaurant, because I couldn't stand ordinary meals," a redheaded woman, starving like all the rest of them, boasts. Then she begins to enumerate all the dishes,

[28] French – a name that is redolent of a rich fragrance. Literally, "a forkful."

151

just the mention of which conjures up marvelous smells and tastes. "For the first course, the waiter would bring us chopped liver in a sauce of shallots, and freshly baked bread of course." Yossel's stomach contracts cruelly. His nostrils tremble at the very thought of the aroma of fried onions. "...and then mashed potatoes, generously flavored with *schmaltz*, and two cutlets, one prepared in the Viennese style, the other in the Jewish style, that is with onions and garlic," she goes on mercilessly, and poor Yossel swallows his saliva. "Usually, as a third course, I would order a roasted goose thigh, and for dessert, a fruit compote," the aristocratic redhead completes the menu. Yossel is about to faint, but he saves the day by calling out loudly: "Missus, have mercy, please stop!"

The policeman directing traffic at the intersection shouts at two people so busy talking they are moving slowly over the pedestrian crossing: "If you want to chatter, do it at Piotrovska.[29] Here we're in the ghetto!" he says in a blunt tone, roughly pushing a man who is swollen with hunger. "Officer," the poor man whimpers, trembling and collapsing on to the sidewalk. He extends his hand towards the policeman and heaps curses upon him: "May your feet swell up! May your face be all puffed up and may you die of hunger!" "Ha, ha, ha!" the cynical policeman, "A real orator I've got here! You might think we've got Rumkowski at his finest here at the podium!" "I hope to see you next to him on the scaffold," the poor fellow responds. "If you go on talking like that, I'll take you to the police station," the policeman threatens, waving his club. "Makes no difference to me, if I'm here or some place else," the living-dead man barks. "So what, so this is how you jeer at

[29] The main street of Lodz.

the ghetto? Does that mean you have a free ticket to the next world?" the policeman goes on, doubling over with laughter…

Avraham Cytryn as a child

The mother, Genia Pik-Cytryn

Daughters of the Cytryn family:
Lucy's grandmother and her
daughters Ruth and Tola and
her granddaughter, Tola's
daughter.

Sarah Dovzhinski, Grandfather
Cytryn's sister

The Cytryn family vacationing at a *pension* in Krinitza, 1936.

The Cytryn family plot in the cemetery

The tombstone on the grave of the father, Yaacov Shimon Cytryn, who died in Lodz

Lucy Cytryn's high school diploma

Work permit issued to Genia Cytryn by the Lodz Judenrat, 1942

The deportation to Auschwitz, the last transport, August 28, 1944. Lucy and her mother are boarding the train, behind them Avraham is carrying a pot over his shoulder.

Jenny Nellie Bialer at the
ceremony where she was
conferred an LLD.

; Filius datus est nob
    Princeps pacis
Venite, adoremus! (Is.9,

    Jan Pawet II papa
  z życzeniami
      i błogosławieństwem
  Brat Karodensi
      1994

The blessing of the Pope,
John Paul II.

160

תעודת הוקרה

תעודת הוקרה זו ניתנת לגב' לוסי ביאלר כהוקרה של העם
בישראל על נדיבותה, מסירותה ללא לאות ותרומתה
החשובה למפעל הציוני

Shlomo Shachar

האפוטרופוס הכללי

Diplôme d'honneur

LE PRÉSENT DIPLÔME D'HONNEUR EST DÉCERNÉ
À MADAME LUCIE BIALER EN TÉMOIGNAGE DE
LA RECONNAISSANCE DE L' ETAT D' ISRAEL
POUR SA REMARQUABLE GÉNÉROSITÉ, DE SON
DÉVOUEMENT SANS LIMITE ET DE L'AIDE
INFATIGABLE QU'ELLE A APPORTÉE À L'
ÉDIFICATION DE L' ETAT D' ISRAEL

Shlomo Shachar

ADMINISTRATEUR GENERAL

Lucy Bialer receiving an honorary
award as a "Woman of Valor" at Yad
Vashem.

Zygmunt (Issak) Bialer

The grave of her grandfather, Abram Eli Pic in Pabienica. Abram
Cytryn was named after him

60th
anniversary
of the
liquidation of
the Lodz
Ghetto,
September
2004

Lucie Bialer presents the Hebrew version of the book to an Israeli
Cantor

Lucie Bialer recites one of her brother's poems to a large audience

162

B. P.
ABRAM CYTRYN
SYN GENI I JAKUBA CYTRYN
ZGINĄŁ W WIEKU 17 LAT
ZA MĘKĘ NARODU
ZA MŁODOŚĆ ZWIĘDŁĄ W SZALE'
ABRAM CYTRYN ZOSTAWIŁ 28 ZESZYTÓW
240 WIERSZY
TABLICE UFUNDOWAŁA SIOSTRA LUCIE
CYTRYN-BIALER JEDYNA OCALAŁA
Z RODZINY. KTÓRA WRACAJĄC
Z OŚWIĘCIMIA ZNALAZŁA W GETTCIE
JEGO ZESZYTY
ת.נ.צ.ב.ח.

Deportation list found by Lucie Bialer at the Radegast train station, includes her mother's and her names

Lucie Bialer stands in front of the wagon in which she was deported from Lodz

Yozik the Shrewd One

Yozik is like a stray dog, always sniffing around. When the ruthless confiscation of Jewish property is discontinued for a time, the clever boy exploits the pause to help out the two sisters he loves very much.

For Chaim Rumkowski, the pause is a relief. During the deportation of the Jews and their transfer to the ghetto, his carriage never stopped traveling back and forth, his telephone never stopped ringing. In brief – the old man nearly went out of his mind. And now, after all that commotion, our man can finally draw a deep breath. The frenzy has calmed down, and our adored king has again taken up the reins of his small, crumbling kingdom.

The gray-haired old man bears the heavy weight of the accursed ghetto on his shoulders. He could easily have gotten rid of it, but it seems he does not really want to. History will reveal to the world what this old man really was. In any event, public opinion is not at all sympathetic towards him. The honorable president is generally considered an easily angered madman, a white-haired devil. Nearly once a year, he moves to another palace, he is given to extreme whims, to fierce outbursts of temper, to stupid manias, to satanic fits.

A wild idea pops into the head of our sly boy. He decides to go speak face to face with His Excellency. He just cannot rid himself of this idea. He goes to the presidential palace and asks the policeman on guard: "Sentry, is the President at home?" The guard looks Yozik over from head to toe and mutters: "What do you want from the old man?" "Take pity on me, I've got a sister who is dying, and

I myself am very ill." "What happened to you?" the curious policeman asks. "Nothing," Yozik replies, confused, "I'm just exhausted and hungry." "I'm hungry too, kid! Get out of here or I'll throw you out!" the policeman extends his arm, a threatening look on his face. Yozik is gone in a second.

The boy could have hung on to the king's carriage, but he did not want to do that, because he had once seen the President slap a man who had climbed on to the step of his carriage. Yes, our adored President is quite prepared to hit miserable residents of the ghetto, even if it arouses everyone's hatred of him. Yozik is as frightened of the presidential hand as he is of fire. What the boy really wants is to find work in a good place – inside a kitchen full of steaming soup, for example. And if all he can obtain is a food coupon, he won't refuse that either. Definitely not!

Yozik is trying to obtain some security and stability in his wretched life, a clearly impossible hope in this human chicken coop, where no one is immune from sudden change.

The ghetto is divided into two groups: the first includes nearly the entire population; the second, only a tiny part – the aristocrats, the blue-bloods, namely, the respected ones, first among them, His Excellence the President. Some others in this group of important persons are Mr. Jakubowicz, the director of the workshops, a quiet, calm man, and Mr. Sheshzevslibi, the ghetto's Minister of Supply, whom everyone regards as a robber and a thief. These epithets, not the most complimentary it's true, have stuck to him so strongly that not even the most charitable deed can rid him of the bad name he has earned. Sheshzevslibi the thief was selected for his job by the people. But is he really happy in that job? With a type like that, how can one know? And should we hold it against him that he takes the greater part of the supplies for himself? Anyone else would do the same, and perhaps even empty out the ghetto's emergency supplies. And there is another dear lady, Miss Dora Fuchs. There are many like her; they are the President's secretaries. In brief, these high-ranking men and women act as masters of the ghetto for a period that varies in length. Because sometimes the wheel turns, and they fall from their lofty positions into the valley of tears. Then they are replaced by other pretenders to the crown, who in their turn climb on to the unstable throne. Generally, those are reckless, lawless, faithless people who exploit the tyranny and the evil and for a while hold the reins of authority. These new crooks sow confusion in the Baluti market, chat with the Germans, look briefly into the offices, hand out orders and punishments, in brief – stand out in every possible way.

Life in the ghetto resembles a carousel on which work, chaos, hunger and despair go round and round in a muddle. Stay in control of yourselves, treat your daily rations with respect and care, don't fall into the abyss of demoralization, try to float on top of the water, those are the basic rules. In the streets of the ghetto, there is a constant bustle, laughter, weeping, a boiling-over, and sometimes a frozen state, a kind of muteness of death. The clogs and the high boots clank on the sidewalks like hammers. The skeletons pass one another, all of them skinny, wretched, pale and sometimes blue or even green. Small children stand at the street corners selling tiny sweets that melt as soon as you put them into your mouth. *"Die groise bombes. Die kletze!*[30] the children call out loudly in unison. The officials hurry to their offices, their briefcases under their arms. People drag sacks of bricks of coal, vegetables, and wood for heating. They drip with sweat, spit, stink, and move on. Scrawny women bow under their burdens, breathing hard, groaning. They push wagons full of clogs arranged in pyramid-like heaps. Sometimes a car goes by in the street loaded with crates of goods, passing rapidly in a cloud of dust that chokes the miserable human-machines of the ghetto. Opposite the Diet Laden, those in charge come to take their special rations, arousing the hatred of the hungry who live only on their meager rations. Chaim Rumkowski's carriage sometimes passes in the street, making a loud clatter. From his lofty seat, the white-haired old man surveys the small plot where work is going on at full speed. When the residents see him, they raise their caps and curtsy. When the carriage disappears around the corner, they mutter curses or jeer at him, imitating his Lithuanian accent. *"Der Kaiser furt."*[31]

Chaim Rumkowski bows his white head in sorrow and is lost in thought. He thinks about the vicissitudes of fate. He himself does not understand how he managed to sail the ship of his fragile life above the stormy waves. Who filled him with this extraordinary energy?

After lunch, the king of the ghetto takes a nap that he definitely deserves. Again and again, he checks to see what time it is. At five he has to go to the Baluti market with Jakubowicz. Then he has to handle some cutbacks in manpower in the kitchens and to assign some young men to the workshops. Production requires new working hands,

[30] Yiddish: "Big candies, as big as bricks."
[31] Yiddish: "The Kaiser is traveling."

doesn't it? Exactly at three, someone knocks at his door shyly. Damn it! The President thinks, Jakubowicz is here. But no, a surprise! Instead of the face he was expecting, the old man sees the fragile silhouette of a boy, standing in the doorway, alternately turning pale and blushing. "*Ver bestu?*"[32] the President asks, stretching his neck to get a better look at his visitor. The boy draws closer and mumbles, "Mr. President, my name is Yozik, I am an orphan." The old man is about to erupt into a fit of rage, but the word "orphan" suddenly softens him. This magic word acts like a tranquillizer on the king's heart. We ought not to forget that before the war, our President, beloved for his good deeds, was very active on behalf of children. He devoted himself body and soul to homeless orphans, hungry children. Everyone knew about this generosity of his. And now a child who has suffered such a bitter fate is standing in front of him. Why shouldn't he come to his aid? Yozik is very aware of this weakness of the President. That's why he dared to appeal to him directly. "You're an orphan, so then you should go to the orphanage. There you can live, eat and sleep, together with other children who share the same fate. Do you agree? You will find plenty of food there and I'll give you a little something extra." Is Yozik satisfied? No, but because he does not want to anger the old man, he stammers softly, "Mr. President, I do not want to go to the orphanage. I do not want to eat or sleep there, because at home I have two little sisters who need me. Mr. President, I would like a place in the kitchen." "What can a lad like you do in the kitchen?" "Eat, Mr. President." The old man bursts into laughter. "You little *mamzer*! You want to shirk and to eat, ah? Do

[32] Yiddish: "Big candies, as big as bricks."

169

you know at least that in the kitchen there is work too? That even a sore throat does not release the worker from the tasks he has to do there?" "I am used to work, Mr. President, I'll be a good worker."

The President looks Yozik up and down and asks him: "How old are you?" "Twelve, Mr. President." "You won't be able to stand the hard work." "I will," Yozik calls out, an insulted look on his face. He strains his muscles and shows them off to the white-haired old man. "Look how strong I am, Sir!" "You are determined to work in one of the kitchens?" "Yes, Mr. President," the boy replies in a shaking voice. The old man goes over to the table, tears a sheet of paper off a notebook, dips his pen in the inkwell and begins to write: To the Kitchen Department. Please immediately accept this boy to work. He adds his signature at the bottom of the page: *Der Elsteste der Juden in Litzmannstadt*,[33] folds the sheet into four and hands it to the boy, who is overcome with joy. "I think that will do," he says. "Go to the kitchen department and give them this paper." Yozik takes the lucky document and kisses the old man's hands. "But just tell me, you naughty boy, how did you manage to get to me?" "It was no problem, Sir. The guard went out to buy a cigarette, and I took advantage of the opportunity." "Very good, and now get out of here," the President says in a paternal tone. The boy thanks him again warmly, and disappears behind the door. The President is once again lost in thought, but his sad mood has disappeared.

Yozik sits on the banister and gaily slides down to the ground floor, where he finds himself face to face with the guard. "You dirty little ragamuffin?" the guard yells, "who

[33] German: Eldest of the Jews (President of the community) in Lodz.

gave you the right to go up there?" Yozik shakes his hand at him dismissively, and shows him the sheet of paper. The astonished guard glances at it, amiably pats the boy on the shoulder and says: "What can I say, you're a lucky one." And Yozik strides proudly down the street, grasping the President's letter in his hand, elbowing his way through the crowd. Now life seems rosy to him. In his mind's eye, he already sees himself sitting in front of a pot full of soup, guzzling it down. I'll gorge myself for a whole week, until no one will be able to recognize me, he thinks. From far away he sees the gate of a building over which hangs a sign *Küchen Abteilung*.[34] The sign draws him like a magnet. He begins to run like a madman. He is afraid that the kitchen department will slip away and disappear under his very nose. He is afraid that some sudden change will destroy his happiness. So he dashes towards the entrance gate, goes into the office section, where a maze of corridors and rooms stretches out in front of him.

Where should I go? Which door should I enter? Who should I ask for? Yozik thinks, and at once he is bending over a wooden partition and placing his paper on the desk of a female clerk who is calmly sitting there. "This is a document from the President himself," the boy says. The woman takes it and throws it into his face. He catches the paper and looks at it in alarm. He turns it over again and again, and then he realizes that both sides of the sheet are empty! There is no sign of a letter, not even one. Oh, woe is me! The poor child trembles and grabs his head with both hands. I've lost the document the President wrote. He runs out of the room like a gust of wind, knocking a girl over on his way out. In the crowded street, his eyes glued

[34] German: Kitchen Management.

to the ground, he begins to sniff like a dog. Nothing! At that same moment, his precious paper, all wet and wrinkled, is floating calmly in the sewage canal. A little further on, there is the opening of a drainage pit. When Yozik suddenly spies his treasure, he jumps desperately towards the sewage. But the satanic current pushes the paper, and it is sucked into the abyss. A catastrophe! It's gone, Yozik yells, and tears the hair from his head. The paper is swallowed up in the sewage. Yozik's shouts alarm the passersby. The boy, disheartened, turns sharply and breaks into a gallop, his head bent. "A *meshugener*,[35] a woman says with compassion. "What a wretched child! So young and already crazy! Another victim of the ghetto!" an emaciated man says. They groan in a chorus, moving away from one another.

After losing the President's letter and his happiness with it, Yozik falls ill. He burns with fever, gets into bed, cries and shivers. After two days of rest, he feels a little better. He begins to fabricate weird plans. The strangest ideas pass through his mind. As soon as he's healthy, he decides to launch another assault on His Excellency the President. He is fortunate in meeting up with the same sentry who was on duty during his first visit. He turns to him with a smile of complicity and reminds him of the presidential adventure he had experienced the last time. After giving it some thought, the sentry utters a long "Aaah!", proof that he hasn't forgotten Yozik's previous visit. A barely discernible wave of his hand, and Yozik is already on the stairs again. He knocks on the door. A deep voice answers him: Come in! and Yozik enters. "Look who it is! You are Yozik, if I'm not mistaken. Why aren't you at work, you idle boy?" "Mr.

[35] Yiddish: "crazy."

President, what a disaster, I lost the paper you gave me, and all of my happiness is gone with it." "You little fool!" the angry old man shouts. "You should have said I sent you, that would have been enough." Yozik lowers his eyes under the severe gaze of the President. "I'll give you a new paper, but this time don't lose it, do you understand?" "Yes, yes," Yozik replies in amazement. "What does that mean, yes, yes?" "No, no," the naïve boy answers. "What does that mean, no, no?" "I won't lose your letter," Yozik explains sweetly and submissively. He opens the door, and at the staircase, gives free rein to his happiness. Again, he slides down the banister, smiles at the policeman on duty, and gallops into the busy street.

After undergoing some more ordeals, Yozik gets a job in one of the kitchens, where he is assigned some simple tasks. He cannot believe his eyes. The kitchen is located in a narrow yard, near a sewing workshop. A young worker adds Yozik's name to the roster of workers. Afterwards, the boy goes into the kitchen, blinded by a cloud of fragrant, tempting steam blowing right into his face from a large pot. Yozik takes a deep breath of the pleasant scent, and at once is assailed by enormous hunger. A bald man, wearing a white chef's hat, stands on the cement sidewalk stirring a boiling pot with a large wooden stick. Someone pushes stunned Yozik, who looks every which way. A stout woman hands the young sous-chef a large platter covered with roasted flour, and rubs her hands with satisfaction. Two soot-covered workers strain to lift a large bowl full of peeled potatoes. They breathe hard and rush about inside the thick clouds of steam.

From the potato-peeling room, a fat woman, her body all swollen, suddenly dashes out. Her huge breasts shake like the weights of a pendulum clock. Yozik, fascinated, cannot take his eyes off her. "Madam," a girl with her sleeves rolled up, calls out, "Do we need to weigh these potatoes now or later?" "Weigh them right now!" the woman in charge roars in a hoarse voice. Yozik has never seen such a woman in all the time he's been in the ghetto. The boy stands in front of her, motionless as a statue, his mouth hanging open, blocking the way from the kitchen to the dining room. "Move!" the heavy-set manageress yells. Yozik, alarmed, jumps aside. The fat woman goes by, and Yozik, amazed, gazes at her impressive buttocks, as they sway to and fro. A smoke-blackened worker goes past and turns to Yozik: "What are you doing here?" "I..," the boy replies, "I've just been accepted to work here." "Then get to work. Roll up your sleeves! You've probably been taken on as a helper. So come help me move this bowl of potatoes to the floor and weigh it." Yozik obediently takes hold of one of the handles, and together with the other worker, lifts the huge pot that they both put down on the scale. Another young man records the weight of the potatoes in a notebook. "Who is that?" Yozik asks his fellow worker, after they've lifted several of these pots. "He's our storekeeper." "And that one?" the curious boy continues, pointing to a short man who is passing by. "That's our boss. They're all ours, the storekeeper, the boss, the daily workers…"

The work they do connects all these people. And what connects their stomachs and hearts is their constant gorging of food. Around the pots, the saucepans, the bowls, stout girls with generous breasts, their sleeves rolled up, dash about, sending their warm, unpleasant breath straight into Yozik's face. It's boiling here! Yozik thinks as he carries, together with a co-worker, a tub full of cold water to the peeling room. "Put it down here!" the young supervisor yells in a hoarse voice. The peelers, sitting on little chairs or stools, work at a feverish pace. They cut the peeled potatoes into pieces, and then throw them into the pots. Nearly all of them have swollen feet that look like wooden posts. Their faces are as round as balls. They are constantly spitting, uttering hoarse cries, boasting, laughing hysterically, whining. In brief, women in the worst sense of the word. Their conversations all revolve around the same subject – food. They talk about soup, about bread, about various delicacies, swallow their saliva, and all that without stopping their work for a minute…

Srul Pakul and Yonye Filitzer

The stomachs of the poor ghetto Jews churn as thick white clouds of steam pour out of the dark opening of the food distribution window.

In front of this window, almost at the gates of paradise, a long line of crazy people wait at the edges of a canal, waving their hands and feet like puppets. A skeletal woman, with a bent nose like a witch's, hurls frightful insults at a small boy called Yonye Filitzer, and shakes her scrawny fist at him. A quarrelsome, troublemaker of a boy, he spares her none of his own vulgar abuse: "May the hole in your ass be plugged up forever! May you swell up like a pumpkin! May your mouth vomit everything it swallows!" The woman, red with rage, shouts back at him. Yonye goes on with his unstoppable flow of insults: "May the teeth you have left fall out and may you be five times as skinny as you are!" "Aye, aye, aye," the woman screeches, and with a determined movement begins banging on the boy's head.

A fight would have broken out, had it not been for the sudden intervention of a man who still possessed a trace of humanity. "How can you behave like that?" he shouts, close to tears. "Don't we have enough trouble?" "It's this rascal's fault, this little bastard snuck into the line!" the woman cries out, sticking her fingers into Yonye's open eyes. "Are you trying to say I wasn't here?" Yonye lies blatantly. "A girl with a red hat and an ugly redhead with freckles were in front of you, and I was here before everyone else." "Get out! Get out!" the people in the line yell. An arrogant old man even brandishes his walking stick at Yonye. A big commotion ensues. The food bowls clatter, feet wearing shoes, clogs and slippers come to life, fists are raised in the air, shouts, curses, moans, groans, whimpers – all jumble together, and the human whirlpool moves towards the window that everyone is yearning to reach. Poor Yonye is forcibly thrown out of the line, and shaking, he rolls into the canal. Mud splatters on the face of this starving wretch, who does not even notice it, because the human herd is trampling on him. "Damn it all," he curses, and launches a frontal assault into the raucous crowd. Someone bangs a pot on his head, and the pain is so intense he sees stars. After fiercely fighting the crowd, he gets to the front and hands his food card to the supervisor. The woman turns her ladle into the large pot, in which several potatoes float on the surface. Saliva fills Yonye's mouth. He swallows it slowly and yells, "Madam, put the ladle down to the bottom, catch me some potatoes!" Ignoring Yonye's recommendations, she serves him the contents of one ladle. "It's not full," Yonye grumbles, stirring the watery liquid in his bowl.

As curious as a cat, Srul Pakul, his neighbor, moves closer and sticks his long nose into Yonye's bowl. Winking at him, Yonye goes on angrily stirring his soup with his sticky spoon. "Look what that dirty fat bag gave me! I hope she explodes with all the soup she guzzles every day!" he cries out bitterly. "If she'd only agree to dip the ladle down to the bottom of the pot," he went on grumbling, "I'd be ready to hug her in my arms, even to kiss her rosy lips! But she's got other fish to fry, she doesn't even look at a wretch like me!"

Yonye's neighbor gets his portion and comes to sit next to him. Their gazes frozen, the two eat, slurping loudly. Afterwards, in unison, they scrape their bowls to get at the last sticky drop.

"Say," Srul asks Yonye in jest, "have you had enough?" Without waiting for an answer, he goes on, red with anger, "If that dirty bitch stays alive after the war… ! If at least the soup would have some effect on me! If only my belly could once be full! If she'd at least give me a normal portion!"

"*Oy vey*!" Yonye complains, "How I miss those good old days!"

"In those good old days," Srul says, "we could have eggs, cheese, buns, milk! Aye, aye, aye!"

"You know, Srul, before the war, I used to go often to eat my fill at Shmul the redhead's place, and boy, what hefty meals I would gobble down! When I think of it, my mouth fills up with saliva. For one zloty, I would get a roast goose thigh with so much garlic and onions that tears would fill my eyes! I'd eat enormous amounts, and of course, there was as much bread as you could eat. My pants would burst, one pair after another, what can I tell you, I had to get bigger size pants. After meals like those, I'd belch and belch with such pleasure. I felt I was truly alive." Srul sits on the step of a dilapidated wooden shanty. He stretches his long thin neck, the neck of a starving person, and in his imagination devours Yonye's goose.

"Srul," Yonye asks him, "why do you look so awful?"

"You idiot! How can you expect me to look good?"

"You just got your ration now, didn't you? At least today you can eat your fill," Yonye teases him. "You're talking rubbish. I have to divide my ration into equal portions," Srul answers sorrowfully. "You're a fool! If you listen to Rumkowski's recommendations, the death wagon will take you to Marysin," Yonye says angrily.

"I'd eat it all up in one go, if my missus didn't watch my

every move," Srul says.

"Do what you feel like, eat as much as you can, and you'll have enough strength to give to others."

Again and again, the shouts from those waiting in line drown out their conversation. Suddenly Srul gets up, hangs his bowl on the belt that is tightly drawn around his scrawny body, and leaves the kitchen with its loud bellows. With every step he takes, the bowl knocks against his backside with a loud bang. A leaden sun beats down mercilessly on the freckled face of this tall, starving Jew. Crushed, wretched and bitter, he passes backyards and heaps of garbage. His stomach is tormenting him, constantly demanding more and more food. The rays of the sun bounce back at him from the windows of the miserable wooden houses. A gang of filthy children, dressed in rags, runs through the streets, speaking among themselves in an ear-splitting jargon, an awful distortion of their language. Lifeless, cowed faces appear at the windows. Heaps of garbage give off disgusting smells, and the sun smites this whole world, turning it into an unbearable furnace.

"*A leben!*"[36] Srul mutters, wiping his sweaty forehead with his hairy hand. "*A churbe! A toit! Oy vey!*"[37] He laments. He climbs the circular staircase and opens the door to his hole-in-the-wall apartment. The stench of excrement grips his throat. Little Eli is sitting on a chamber pot, concentrating so hard that his eyes nearly pop out of his head.

"Can't you go outside to shit?" Srul yells at his son, who tenses his body even more and opens his eyes wide.

[36] Yiddish: "What a life!"
[37] Yiddish: "Catastrophe! Death! Woe!"

"I didn't want to let him go out!" his wife Chava shouts from the smoke-blackened kitchen. "You know very well that this wild kid of ours was sick!"

"If you don't let him go out to get some air, he'll stink up the whole house! The weather's pleasant now, kids are playing outside, he ought to be out there with them, instead of staying here alone!" Srul shouts back.

Alarmed, little Eli gets off the pot. He is terrified of his father's fits of temper.

"Did you get our rations?" Srul suddenly asks Chava.

"Yes," she replies. "There were so many people there, and what a holy mess!" "Listen, Chava, give me my portion of sugar and jam now," her husband asks.

"What, do you think I'm stupid? What will you do, eat it all up in one day and then walk around with your tongue hanging out? I've already been through that once," Chava protests.

"But listen, dear, if I ask you for my portion, what right do you have to refuse me?"

"Srul, stop making a big deal out of everything! I'll give you your daily ration."

Chava places the scale on the table, weighs out her husband's portion and gives it to him. A plate full of sugar and another full of jam are now sitting in front of him, making his mouth water. Chava's eyes seem to be warning him not to touch the plates. He tastes a small teaspoon of sugar, slyly, and then one of jam, and concludes that if he eats it all at one go, the world won't end. The jam that looks so innocent is pulling at him like a magnet. A brilliant idea suddenly pops into his head: "Eat your bread ration and you'll be in good shape for at least one day." He gets up, with trembling steps goes over to the cupboard and takes out his loaf of bread. Chava sees him and cries out:

"You miserable wretch, aren't you afraid of God? What are you doing?" "I want to give myself a good shot of vitamins," Srul replies. "So you'll die of hunger afterwards?" Srul cuts the bread into thick slices, spreads jam and then sugar on them, and begins eating. "You're mad!" his despairing wife yells, and grabs the remainder of the bread. "Give it to me!" Srul screams, as his mouth begins to fill with saliva. "You fool! What will you eat tomorrow and the next day?" she yells furiously. "Tomorrow, I'll swallow my anger, and the next day I'll go to Marysin, or the war will end!"

Srul suddenly tears the bread from Chava's hands, and in a fury, crumbles it. Breathing hard, he sits back down and starts eating again. Chava goes over to her husband in a fighting mood, holding an iron food grinder in her left hand.

"Chava, if you touch me, I'll kill you!" "At least leave two slices for tomorrow's breakfast, or I'll tear this place apart!"

Srul is terrified of the heavy weapon his wife is holding, having already felt its effect in the past. What a disaster! He had intended more than once to throw that piece of iron into the rubbish, but afraid of his wife's temper, he had given up on that idea…

Moishe the Snitch

The tenants of the building in Zbozowa Street are racking their brains – they want to know why Moishe Obersohn looks good and his wife is getting as big as a barrel. How to explain this happy change? The wretched couple was already really deteriorating physically, and now, suddenly – it began just seven weeks ago – their faces have become more placid, their nerves are less frazzled, and their mood is greatly improved. Perhaps they are swollen because of hunger? the tenants think, passing them by again and again, trying to guess from their faces the reason for this sudden stroke of good luck. There's no question about it, they've put on fat and now look like the well-fed notables.

In the yard, in the stairway, the gossip passes in a flurry. One malicious neighbor claims he saw Moishe going into the *Kriminalpolizei*.[38] One small spark like that is enough to get everyone's tongues clacking – Moishe is an informer. People begin keeping their distance from him. The street urchins point to him from afar. When Moishe draws closer, all the secret conversations stop, and people switch to a completely neutral subject. The contemptible squealer still keeps on greeting his neighbors politely and telling them funny stories. Instead of touching on the awful, inevitable subject of food, he brings up more soothing subjects that have nothing to do with eating. But what is going on with Obersohn? His stomach cannot be content with the miserable rations that the President is allotting us! Is it possible that he has given up his self-respect for the sake of the pleasure of gorging himself?

[38] German: The criminal police.

This business is driving Moishe's poor neighbors crazy, in particular Yonye Pzetak and his beloved, gossipy wife. "Tell, me, Shura," he asks her again and again, "how come Moishe's face is glowing like that? He's an informer, I'm hundred per cent sure of that!" "*Oy, vey!*" the respectable woman cries out, "Don't talk to him any more about politics. He'll probably inform on you to the *Kriminal-polizei*, and then we'll really be in trouble!"

From that day on, Yonye Pzetak refuses to converse with his dangerous neighbor. When Moishe comes close to Yonye and asks him jovially, "So, what's up, Yonye, what's new?" the latter just seals his lips or shrugs his shoulders.

A Coffee Torte

There's also some joy in the wretched homes of the Jews. A ration of two kilograms six-hundred grams of potatoes is nothing to be sniffed at! You can fry them, or throw them with a glowing face into the pots. The Jews have learned an important chapter in gastronomy. Right now a culinary discovery is making the rounds in the ghetto, stirring up a storm. Shimsi Korchak asks Yente, the queen of cooks, to explain what he has to do to prepare the wonderful recipe for the coffee torte.

"Take about one half kilo of potatoes, peel them and grate them fine. Pour two tablespoons of black coffee, two tablets of saccharine, and a heaped tablespoon of flour onto the mixture, and blend it all well," Yente proclaims.

"And then?" Shimsi asks, holding his breath. "If you add a drop of vanilla or rum extract, it will be even better. Then take a small pot, grease it with a drop of oil and pour the mixture in. Cover the pot well and place it inside a bigger pot of boiling water, and cover that too. An hour and a half later, turn the cake over on a plate. And believe you, me, you'll have a torte just like before the war, the kind of delicacy they used to serve in Zimianska's coffee house.

Korchak, excited by this wonderful invention, takes a whole kilogram of potatoes, grates them, adds four heaped tablespoons of coffee, two tablespoons of flour, and five pieces of saccharine, and carefully follows all of Yenta's instructions. He impatiently keeps gazing at the pot, becoming intoxicated by its wonderful fragrance. Oy, he thinks, a real cake for the Sabbath! He turns the torte over on a plate, sprinkles a little sugar on it, and his lovely family bolts down the tasty delicacy.

When it comes to culinary and domestic affairs, there's equality between the sexes. The man knows no less than the woman, and the woman is no less interested than the man. Turnip cakes, chopped cabbage liver, radish onions! All of these substitutes that deceive the stomachs of the ghetto residents, are now well known to Korchak.

Yente's new recipe has somewhat expanded his gastronomic horizons. So now, the coffee torte made of potatoes is making its appearance in the show windows of the stores, where it is sold as if it were a luxury item.

A Wonder Drug

Three years in the confines of the ghetto, deprived of fats and vitamins, can only have a harmful effect on the physical and mental development of the residents. The first symptom: weakness of the legs and general fatigue. Then the illness spreads. Strangely enough, the legs become paralyzed. But since the illness is limited at first, people don't take it seriously. Then there is a significant increase in the number of afflicted Jews. The doctors take an interest, and their diagnosis is a lack of calcium in the bones because of a deficiency of fatty substances and vitamins. It turns out that it is a real epidemic.

A policeman directing traffic in the ghetto is suddenly attacked by this awful disease and is unable to walk. Clerks who spend their days keeping complicated accounts suddenly find their legs growing numb, and they begin to walk like children taking their first steps. The disease does not spare the workers either.

A catastrophe! What can be done? A huge question mark hangs over the ghetto as the dreadful epidemic takes its effect on larger and larger segments of the community. An ominous curvature distorts the bones, and they seem about to shatter with a loud, cry crack. But one fine day, what a miracle! A Jew takes a wonder drug, and his paralyzed legs become alive again as if they were touched by a magic wand. His blood begins to flow normally again, and his legs are able to walk, jump, run. A real miracle! Vignato! The rumor spreads quickly. A wonder drug that cures and revives numb legs! Vignato! A health oil, the reviving medication that saves people from the fatal paralysis and enables them to get through the war!

If you only can, save yourself! As soon as the news hit the street, hundreds of Jews already…

The Border-Smuggling Dog

Something so amazing has just happened. The Jewish policeman stands there open-mouthed, while the German soldier has lost his balance. A dog from the other side of the city has just leaped over the barbed wire fence to visit the ghetto. Even the most skilled smuggler would not have risked his life the way that dog has, just because he suddenly missed onions and garlic.

Oh, my boy, your canine sense of smell has misled you! The good days are gone forever! Now we live in the most pitiful poverty. But this is a particularly sun-drenched day. As the dog runs about, he stirs up a golden cloud of dust, blinding the furious soldier, who mutters a curse, "*Donnerwetter*" – thunder and lightning!

The Jewish policeman, as skinny as a stick, shakes with fear, but he still tries to maintain the respectable demeanor his job demands. "Why didn't you try to catch the dog when I lost my balance?" the German soldier asks in an aggressive tone. The emaciated Jew straightens up and replies in a whining voice, "Because…because I couldn't keep my balance either, and it was galloping as if it had gone mad."

The soldier moves his rifle from one shoulder to another and takes shelter in his sentry box. Neither he nor the Jewish policeman noticed the object the smuggler-dog was carrying between his teeth. But others did. The crowd took notice of the precious chunk that the dog was about to devour.

After he crossed over the barbed wire fence, the dog disappeared into an alley, on both sides of which stood squalid wooden houses. "A dog with meat!" a gossipmonger cries out from her window, and at once throws a stone at the small animal, which hits the house opposite and falls silently onto the sidewalk. A man, his food bowl banging against his backside, chases after the dog. A schoolboy, playing with dice on the sidewalk, straightens up, and armed with a stick, rushes after the man. A freckled child grabs his mother's sweater and yells excitedly: "Mama, look, the dog has what looks like half a kilo of meat in his mouth, everyone's running after him!" Despite their leaden legs, all the passersby, yelling, run along with the dog who heroically defends his precious piece of meat. The poor thing never thought he would attract so many eyes or stir up so many stomachs. He drops one ear submissively, while the second remains erect. His teeth have sworn not to let go of the meat, no matter what.

Very soon the entire street and its surrounding area are on the alert. The sensational news arouses the hunting instinct among some Jews. The rumor spreads like a trail of dust: an Aryan dog, white with black spots, has deceitfully entered the ghetto holding a treasure in his mouth.

At an intersection, the dog loses his sense of direction. From all sides, flocks of hungry people assail him. The poor beast is dreadfully anxious, fearing the mob will mercilessly slaughter him. But the hunk of veal, giving off a terrible stink, gives him back his courage. If only I could find a quiet corner to eat my delicacy! the poor dog thinks. How bad have things become that not even a dog is allowed to eat in peace? A shame! A disgrace for people who think they are smarter, superior creatures. He takes a leap backward, and hardly touching the ground, flees with his loot in his mouth. The doorman at one of the sewing shops leaves his post, caught up in the large flow and joins the chase. "What's going on?" he asks the passersby. "A dog has stolen a piece of meat!" dozens of hungry men and women cry in unison. The poor animal is now in a dreadful position – the menacing mob is drawing closer to him, ready to grab him and tear the meat out of his mouth.

With one last bound, the dog leaps into an office, frightening the white-faced clerk, who falls from his chair, holding his pen in his hand. The dog finds shelter in a corner of the office, and quickly begins devouring the piece of meat. The mob wants to break down the door of the office, but the furious clerk pushes them away, slamming the door in their faces. Another, braver clerk, tries to knock the meat out of the dog's mouth with a large knife. The dog, open-eyed, follows the man's movements, and utters a menacing growl. Unfortunately, the clerk fails to take note of the threat, and when he repeats his movement, the dog bites him on the leg. Pale and stunned, the man lets go of the knife, which drops on the floor with a loud bang. The dog flees through the service door that leads to the yard.

The red piece of meat, torn courageously from the dog's jaw, now lies in the corner of the office, tempting the clerks. After the storm of emotions subsides, one of them grabs the meat greedily and wraps it in a piece of paper. "You'll be able to make yourself a royal feast. This time you got a live coupon, not a paper one!" a very envious colleague of his congratulates the lucky man.

The dog, his ears lowered and his tail between his legs, wanders about the streets of the ghetto. When he arrives at the barbed wire fence, he stops. Leave this place, where no one shows any hospitality and everyone gave you such a hard time! he says to himself. And at once he jumps over the fence and with a bleak look, takes leave of the land of shame and poverty.

Sherlock Holmes of the Ghetto

The Jewish police of the ghetto does its work well. The streets are full of colorful police caps with Stars of David on them. Their work is carried out with respect for the hierarchy, and strict, but not too rigid, discipline. Since the ghetto's establishment, many varied changes have been made to improve the life of the Jews. Opposite the Baluty market, there is a police post, the *Ordnungsdienst*, usually guarded by two very noisy guards.

As we usually say, the stars in the sky come out twinkling one after another, but they do not resemble one another. The star of a man called Gertler, for example, has just soared in the ghetto, and it lights up the heavens with its bright rays. Gertler energetically commands a small unit of policemen known as *Sonder*. He very quickly imposes his authority on the ghetto notables. His office is located in an attractive building at 96 Zgierska Street, whose windows overlook the barbed wire fences, behind which cars, trams and carriages harnessed to horses, drive by.

Not far from the *Sonderabteilung*, there is a passageway through which the Jews cross the street. A Jewish policeman directs the traffic. Anyone wishing to cross has to get into line and wait submissively for a sign from the German soldier, who signals that the way is clear. Passengers on the trams on Zgierska Street can enjoy a view of the ghetto from both sides of the street. From time to time, the German soldier signals with his hand or his head, the Jewish policeman yells, and the crowd crosses the street. Afterwards the trams, cars and carriages began to move again. And so it goes, one day after another, without a stop.

In the spring or on warm summer days, the windows of the *Sonderabteilung* stay wide open, and through them you can see the faces of the *Sonder* workers, some of whom look like boys. A sweet melody or a tune that sounds like a complaint sometimes comes from there. There is a sort of mental moroseness in youth, and the rustle of the leaves respond to it like an echo.

The police post overlooks a yard, and the guard from the *Sonder* unit whistles a gay tune. Offices and yet more offices. Pictures of the commander hang on the wall, alongside photographs of the President. Cutouts, drawings, illustrations, notices, notes, orders, and the management's recommendations: Don't spit on the floor, cleanliness means life, stay calm, and the like.

The row of offices, windows, counters, a journal in which the names of all those holding meal tickets are recorded, the main office, the waiting room, the cloak-room, the guardroom, the night guards, etc.

A cheerful atmosphere prevails in the conference room of the *Sonder* unit. One happy fellow, whose cap lies sideways on his head, hums a light tune, and his comrades, standing or sitting on easy chairs, listen to him:

> Once upon a time there was a *Sonder*
> Who got mad as hell
> The lightning got the best of him
> Rumek left him empty
> The prison finished him off,
> Until he shat in his pants…

"Once there was a *Sonder*," his friends reply in the refrain. Then a policeman bursts out singing another song, and the whole group begins laughing jovially. The commander arrives, issues an order, and the policemen leave the room. Silence.

The thieves, robbers and looters are in dread of Gertler's policemen. They uncover and thwart every plot. Gertler is a second Sherlock Holmes. He has a will of iron and a noble heart. Here come the police! The whisper goes around the streets of the ghetto.

A dirty scheme has just been uncovered in one of the bakeries. The manager arranged with his workers to hide a twenty-kilo sack of flour. Someone informed on them, and the gang was caught. Two *Sondermen* come to arrest the disgraceful criminals. They are brought to trial and jailed in the prison on Czernaiski Street.

From then on, a man from the *Sonder* unit begins supervising the distribution of potatoes. The policemen escort the vehicles that bring the vegetables. In the kitchens, soup is served under the watchful eye of the guards. *Sonder, Sonder!* The number of shams – big and small – is on the decrease.

The manager of one of the kitchens stands guard, afraid that a nasty policeman will show up and stick his nose into the soup distribution. A guard at the dairy spills white cheese into a small pot and disappears secretly into a nearby room, where he greedily gulps down his loot.

Suggestions and requests pour into Gertler's office endlessly. The second-in-command to the king of the Litzmannstadt ghetto, the patron of the poor, the generous policeman – hands out cards right and left. "Long live Gertler!" the crowd cheers. Out with those swindlers who are in charge of supplies! Long live justice!" Here you needed some pull and there you needed some influence. But all that's over! The *Sonder's* activity is constantly expanding, to the sorrow of the ghetto's thieves, who were in the habit of exploiting the quiet times to fill their inventory.

Gertler has introduced a semblance of order into the economic life of the ghetto. He has helped improve the daily life of the starving population. He has imposed a strict system of regulations that enabled the ghetto to rid itself of so much corrupt activity.

The *Abruchstelle*

The *Abruchstelle* is in charge of destroying certain buildings in the ghetto. Because these buildings are so high, the work on them is difficult and dangerous. Workers, filthy from head to toe, spread out on the roofs and carry out the task of destroying the ghetto. The plaster is crumbling, and heaps of debris are already turning to dust. Hammers are pounding on the old Polish façades and the air is thick with the dust of bricks. It's painful to draw a breath, but the walls won't give in. Sometimes, with a supreme effort, the workers manage to push over a wall, which collapses with a roar.

It is painstaking work that calls for a great deal of perseverance. The hands of the Jewish workers are often bloody. Their lives, harder than rock, are marked by despairing monotony. Exhausted and crushed, they knock down the buildings, piece by piece.

Who is sent to these demolition sites? The Jews whose physical condition is at its lowest ebb or the wretched ones – those who do not have "long hands," as people say in jest, meaning, those who have no one among the privileged residents who can arrange easier jobs for them. At dawn, an army of weary workers goes out to work. They arrive at the demolition site with a sense of submission. They are young, but they look petrified, nearly dead. Each of these masks bears the imprint of suffering and torture. Their gazes are inscrutably deep, like a riverbed that has dried up, as they glance with terror in every direction. These men walk at a turtle-like pace, moving ahead only when they are pushed. If they were left alone, they would spread out on the heaps of ruins and sleep peacefully. They tuck their shoulders into the worn-out collars of their jackets or coats. Their heads always bent, they are motionless within the emptiness, petrified and shrouded in grief. Beasts of labor. The expression, "an army of workers" does not suit them, because it implies sturdy figures, shaking the earth under their masculine stride.

Who are they, in fact, these workers? Tiny fish, beasts, broken vessels, part of the familiar crowd of living dead in the ghetto. In a certain sense, they are brothers of the coarse, bestial savages that spit on themselves and speak in a despicable, animal-like dialect, a sound that grates on your ears. They so distort words that their sentences sound like formless lava. Some, instead of using hammers, use dull tools, pounding at the stone with abysmal despair.

One side of Brzezinska Street has already been completely demolished. Red bricks are piled up on the ground. Here and there, the workers have built small pyramids of debris. Brzezinska Street was once one of the biggest, most interesting streets of the Lodz ghetto. A huge straw-processing workshop was located in the houses numbered 86 and 88. There was bustling life behind the dreary gray walls. Loud noise and the sound of many workers always echoed from it. In the yard, women dragged large braids of straw to a destination known only to them. Sometimes a wagon from the Baluti market drew up before the entry gate of the workshop. The driver would lash his whip and shout to the porter to open the gate. The wagon would be parked in the yard, opposite the shoe warehouse, and the filthy workers would load merchandise on it, load after load, like stylized pyramids. Later the wagon would leave the area and drive to the market.

The wagons would arrive one after the other into the yard of the workshop, and when they finished loading, would return to the Baluti market. On their way, they passed the gloomy skeletons of buildings, where small groups of workers were moving about. Then the wagons would turn into Lagiewnicka and back to the market.

Every piece of earth in the ghetto is full of hustle and bustle. The dynamics of production is usually a sign of power and health. But the workers in the workshops were producing at the expense of their health. They were both producing and destroying at the same time. The *Abruchstelle* demolishes the buildings, and Glazer's workshops organize elegant fashion shows. The most beautiful creations, the most sublime products, and the most degrading humiliations – all these alternately illuminate and stain the accursed ground of the ghetto.

The War

When night falls, the inhabitants of the ghetto draw their black curtains so the light won't filter into the street. And when thick darkness covers the houses, the beams of the German projectors trace the star-filled skies, searching for the enemy. Then they disappear. The ghetto sleeps, cramped in the leaden sleep of the miserable.

The nighttime hours are usually the sweetest, because they tear the Jews away from the sorrow and sadness of the reality. But the truth is that even as they lie under their warm blankets, sleeping and snoring, in their dreams they see pictures of horror and catastrophe. The hell of the daily dramas seeps into their nightmares, turning into horrific scenes. Sometimes the night – the good, noble friend, the safe shore of quiet, forgetfulness and peace – wears the form of shadows, masks and tragic ghost stories, and becomes a chaos of despair too, tormenting thoughts and feelings. It's agonizing for them. What Jew does not dream of a white, soft roll, still warm, of trays heaped high with slices of cake, of fruit, meat and vegetables? In their sleep, the wretched of the ghetto experience the pleasure of nutrition. But when they awake, the golden sights vanish, and the cruel reality strikes them in the face like the blinding, gloomy light of dawn.

The street lamps waver slightly in the night wind, dropping their murky shadows on the cracked walls. The silence of death imbues everything. Snowflakes flutter like diamonds in the light of the lamps. A full, round moon emerges between the clouds, lighting up the ruins. It's not the first time the moon has looked upon this hell. On several occasions it has sent its silver rays into streams of hot blood, into bodies lying in heaps, in open wounds, the twitches of torment, fires, smoke ash! This war is the handiwork of one barbarian and a million thoughtless soldiers, hypnotized by a tyrant.

Fascism, imperialism, these venomous ideas, have blackened the land – the divine fruit. They have gouged at it and burrowed in it, and eroded the vital roots that feed it. The destructive work of fascism, which has so impassioned the Germans, will lead to the end of the world, or perhaps a flower will bud from the ashes, the flower of renewal, that will entirely change human civilization. Is there anything to be gained from this horrific, mechanical war that strikes like lightning? Unquestionably, the war is a law of nature. A new era will spring from the vestiges of the monstrous hydra, progress will flourish, and there will be no more horror. Humanity is wallowing in the abyss of infamy; it feeds on bestial passions, stormy outbursts, mad, tragic scenes. Humanity lives, humanity creates. From the ruins, a new era will flower, and from it will spring culture and progress. The twists and turns of the globe develop creativity and art. Art develops beauty and sublimity. Beauty and sublimity lead to perfection. And from perfection, God is born.

AVRAHAM CYTRYN

POET

We

Before we can come to an understanding, first of all we need to get to know one another. That's a prerequisite for criticizing each other's work and for perceiving how our minds work as we create. We are not devoting enough attention to what we are. The creative work is no less important than the creator's personality.

Sometimes a genius artist tries to rouse his fellow writers but gets no encouragement at all from them. When that happens, he allows himself to despair, convinced that he is worthless. Nonetheless, the true, original work requires an enormous effort. How many critical reviews and how much suffering until he finally gains recognition! The authentic, unique work is always born in blood, and it improves and is perfected over time. Our talents are still closed inside buds, and we must create an atmosphere that is more than vain chatter, one that is capable of shaping our thoughts and spirits.

I regret the fact that our meetings until now[39] were filled with idle talk. Our president is a wonderful person, but unfortunately, she is not suited to her office. She has a grating voice and a tendency to sew disorder. Neither Czikyert nor Risio nor I are capable of filling this position. I think Matek Rotenberg is the only one who fits the bill, because of his calm, authoritative nature and his practical thinking. Some of our members, Czikyert, for example, regard our club as an added activity, secondary in importance, and they are not far wrong in thinking that. Czikyert is an alert, clever fellow who perceives our

---

[39] Avraham Cytryn was a member of a poets club that met regularly.

meetings as chaotic, a big mess, so he doesn't bother to become involved in our group activities.

Since we want to create something serious, we must work together to correct all of our shortcomings. After all, we are a family of artists, and our mutual understanding should turn us into a close-knit group.

I

I take life to heart. Everything that happens to me I experience passionately. A strong, enormous love that pulls me into the most secret recesses of the human soul compels me to write.

Sometimes it is actually hate that ignites the fever of creativity in me. Because I am as extreme in love as I am in hate. To love and hate. Two forces that turn me into an angel or a devil. Two dictates that control my life, my most precise and strongest stimuli. What despair! Why am I so inclined to have such feelings and thoughts? Why am I suddenly caught up in such bursts of creativity, and then sink at once into the depths of hell? Am I destined to live in such extremes and to constantly move from one pole to another? From one terrible idea to another? I search for the truth and for its awful meaning. Sometimes I suffer from that, but sometimes it's imposed on me; it is my brain, so hungry for knowledge that pushes me. It is probably my destiny to probe the soul of man and to compare it to my own. Why does no one understand me? I myself don't understand myself, and despite all my efforts, I cannot manage to plumb the depths of the chaos in my soul, which is dominated by turbulent emotions.

The emotions. That hidden thread that links me to the star-studded heavens, to the illuminating blue, to compressed, whispering nature. To what is above and beyond, to God Himself, to the supreme spiritual tension. From my face, it is not hard to decipher my thoughts and feelings. Anger and hatred smolder inside me and forcibly erupt, like lava bursting from the crater of a volcano, to destroy, to crush. And then once again, my face is suffused with a peaceful calm that engulfs my heart like a healing balm. When night falls, descending straight from the heavens, it wraps me in its pleasant thoughts, thoughts as light as the rustle of angels' wings.

Every day and every hour leave their marks on my soul, and these repeated experiences, be they bitter or sweet, are engraved in my memory as if they were sacred. Some of these memories are so painful, it seems nothing can ever erase them. I have had many dreadful experiences that have seared my soul like a blazing fire. With so much pleasure I recall my childhood! How dear it is to my heart! I remember the day when our servant locked me in a huge, dark room in order to punish me. Fear aroused my nightmarish fantasies. In my mind's eye, I go back and see myself, small, pale, shaking, all curled up in a corner, turning the mahogany breakfront into a terrifying monster moving its frightening antennae. In my imagination, the room became an inferno filled with scarecrows, products of my anxiety. My first poem, a childhood poem, was the first, fragile expression of my inspiration. I recall my life as a small child, a life of sweetness, lightheartedness, and the joyful secrets of childhood. I recall the hikes, the trips, the plans, and many, many stronger emotions. The enthusiasm, the sallies into the past. And the battles of Napoleon too that I repeated with my classmates: a pillow on the head, a stick in the hand, and the brave general is already in the heat of battle! A roaring voice, supposedly Napoleon's, and a speedy movement of the stick intended to arouse my friends at play – the Emperor's great army - to join the battle. I can once again see that scene with amazing clarity. What a rush of emotions washed over me when I placed my hand behind my back, in that gesture so typical of Napoleon! How noble and proud; I felt that I was in control of the world! I was Napoleon, I was his likeness, I had revived his soul. For me, as I waved the stick and gazed in the distance towards the battlefield, it was not a game. In my eyes, my friends were truly the Emperor's soldiers. When they fell in battle, they were truly dead. And then came the defeat. With bowed head, my Napoleon walked through the rooms, a gloomy expression on his face, his eyes glued to the floor that was now a snow-covered plain. Smitten with sorrow, I delivered a speech to the remnants of my large army. My soldiers looked at me with a smile tempered with a touch of mockery. It is hard to describe in words my pain and suffering. I slapped an old soldier. Later I had to appear before the dreadful caricature of the school principal and take my punishment.

I pass over my life with hellish speed, wrapping in silence scenes, details, moments of depression and ardor, which are meaningful to me but hard to describe in writing. I am postponing for later my plan to describe my life in several volumes: "My Childhood," "My Youth," and so on. Dear God! How many tears have I spilled, how many ordeals have taken their toll on my fragile existence! How many deviations from the high road have led me into dark labyrinths! How many fatal emotions have I experienced, how many drives to take my own life, how many depressions, how many outbursts of enthusiasm! These two extremes dart around inside me all the time, struggling against one another with growing intensity. What will happen when the tension rises too high? An explosion, or the opposite – calmness and dulled senses? I am confronted by a mystery: who am I? A dreamer, philosopher, artist, criminal, deviant, a storm, pleasant weather, a sun, twilight, endless chaos – an inner voice answers me. God – what will happen to me?

The Madness of Mankind

Hurry my brethren! Let us join together!
We shall drown life in blood,
Poison a universe with lethal gas
We will destroy lands, one by one.
European civilization passes by a
Pile of corpses, pyramids of bodies.
Let us expose our madness!
Veteran soldiers, peasants of steel
Let us embrace in a turbulent whirlpool
The bayonets glitter in our eyes,
The greedy, craven land
Is immersed in a pool of blood
And all the clods of earth
Are stained by swathes of steaming scarlet
And the world, like a vast grave
Sinks into the abyss of annihilation

The War

The cannons smoke, glittering.
The soldiers are paralyzed with fear.
Innocent civilians are terrified.
Rifle bayonets riddle them.
A grenade shrieks, falls, explodes.
A man runs, stops, crouches.
The wind blows furiously, lightning strikes.
Another explosion, a cloud, flashes.
Silence! The street freezes, somber.
Explosion, smoke, lightning.
A building collapses.
Screams!
A blood-red light ignites the heavens.
A confused crowd.
The smell of fire, heaps of debris, blazes.
Tracks broken in two, an isolated station,
A fallen pole, a roll of barbed wire,
Testimony to a dangerous calm.
Railway cars lying on their side
Halting the march of the refugees
Eyes scan the pure-white clouds.
A change of the guard, loud steps of soldiers.
In the vast heavens, a bang, a snort.
An officer yells at the top of his lungs:
Achtung! Everyone cringes.
The officer trembles, pale as chalk,
And above, a bomber springs from between
the clouds,
A black swastika painted on its body.

Hidden in the woods, a cannon fires a shell.
Dark smoke masks the blue skies.
It drops from the clouds with a splendid flame,
Turning and twisting like a feverish top.
A wireless message! Lost!
The crowd repeats the name. The war! The
war!

The Battle of the Eagles

Two birds, two eagles, lie in wait for one
another
Circling, spinning in the calm skies,
Attacking, swooping down on their prey,
Slicing the heart of the clouds like cannon
shells.
The motors roar, the airplanes hurtle.
Joy, sun, pleasure.
But the pilot, tense and blue-faced
Does not smile.
The wings tremble in the flight,
The faint melody trembles in one voice with
The iron nerves of the pilot.
Ah! One climbs higher and higher!
Ah! The other dives into the depths!
The motors groan! The guns rattle!
Down below the mob flees, dying, growing
blue.
Turns, circles, half circles, flights!
Drops of sweat flow from the parachute
A play of nerves, play of eagles, a struggle unto
death.
With dawn they meet
In the blue skies, in the gust of the wind.
The clouds clear up, the sun laughs.
The plane wavers from side to side.
 Death spasms, bright flashes.
The engine dies, a column of smoke bursts
forth

Sending the plane to the abyss of eternity
The sun becomes transparent and glowing.

The Cheerful Pessimists

Dear friends! To hell with sorrow
What does it have to do with youth?
Pessimism is worthless.
Dear friends! Not every day can we laugh.
Off with you, sorrow, long live joy!
Leap, turn, move!
Throw your pains and bad habits into the rub-
bish heap.
We are cheerful pessimists,
Youthful, as light as the wind.
Hurrah to youth, long live joy, and to hell with
all the rest!
Life is fleeting and filled with dangers.
So let us remain united forever.
He who has drained the cup of misery
Will be plagued by fear all his life.
Let joy intoxicate us into forgetfulness
Let us forget our suffering and troubles
Off with you sorrow that stymies our hearts.

Funeral

They lift, laboriously drag
A normal body on a normal board.
Behind the stretcher, a procession of white-
faced Jews
Silence and darkness!
The lamp sheds a miserly light.
At the entrance, a Jew sobs, a woman
Wrings her frozen, emaciated hands.
The wretched life of the ghetto exposes teeth
Black tangled hair flies in the wind.
The whiteness of the street is frozen in the
silence.
The Jewish witch lays her hand
On her forehead, and sobs.
The stretcher slides into the open pit.
Finished!
With two, the work goes faster.
The skull of the dead man swings.
A cat's eyes glow at a distance.
And the death wagon is moving away
Swallowed up in the dark abyss of the ghetto.
The mother remains alone with her terrible
suffering.
The black wagon vanishes
And all around, everything is lifeless.
Only the moans resonate.
What has happened?
She asks the emptiness.
And suddenly she clasps her hands

A terrified look
The silence of death has petrified her.
A stone crushes her heart
A stream of blood flows from her wound
The cold penetrates her.
Standing, a look of madness
The Jewish witch stares all around.

An Unforgettable Day

From the depths of the gloomy ghetto
The mad poet leaped.
His eyes glistening,
The satanic, divine creature ran
And sat upon the strange earth to write.
His hair as kinky as an African's
He cries forth like a devil,
In rhymes, tells a few horrific stories,
As if intoxicated by the fumes of alcohol
He rhymes "youth" with "truth."
What is happening here, upon the earth?
The sun wanders among the ruins, laughing.
The body is riddled with the bullets of Europe.
The tyrant of the world crouches deep in the
ground
Hoping perhaps, still hoping
To flog the despicable world.

Love between the Barbed Wire Fences

Love knows no boundaries
Love sneers at barriers
The words 'dear' and 'beloved'
Possess wondrous, secret powers.
The barbed wire of Litzmannstadt separated them
But iron cannot come between hearts.
Each day, a man and a woman
Secretly passed by the German soldier
She handed him a decorated basket
And he took the package with joy
She showed him her passionate love
And on his lips she placed a kiss.
Thus, each day they would meet
Anxiously gazing at the darkness beyond the fence.
And one fine day he told her earnestly
They'd no longer be able to love one another.
But why? The surprised young woman whispered
Why can't our love continue?
If you wound my aching heart
I will never stop weeping and sobbing.
Your kiss is a fine gift for me,
The weary young man went on to say,
And it does not confound or harm me,
But in its place, I prefer your basket
That draws me to come to the barbed wire fence.

How can I love you, my dearest
With the passion of beautiful Apollo
When my stomach is as empty as a dry well
And my soul is like a barren tree?

Litzmannstadt Ghetto

I will never forget you
Litzmannstadt Ghetto.
I will never forget
The mournful contours of your wire fences.
I see you! Mother! Woman!
For you, the world no longer exists!
Nightmare, with your weight you crush the
ghostly shadows!
Litzmannstadt Ghetto.
A land imprisoned
In the claws of the fences.
A snippet of decaying life!
Stinking rot,
Sullied for years.
Co-op, laden, hunger, etc. A world.
A grave, a tombstone upon it.
Sick humanity emits a moldy smell.
Wandering souls, stuck in the mud.
A mob immersed in blood and sweat.
Machines making infernal noise.
Feverish death endlessly harvesting.
A snippet of life stained with original sin.
The agonies of the ghetto, a hanging tongue, a
tormented belly.
The potatoes have arrived,
A new wave of rejoicing.

Life, Madness

Why live? To live.
Why rot? To rot.
I digest the indigestible leftovers of my life.
Towards the light, the darkness, the face turns.
I borrow the tiger's predatory claws
Grab hold of my life and devour it.
From the tainted meat blood flows
A bitter piece sticks in my throat
I resolutely go on with my meal
The meat bleeds.
I bite like a wild beast who's fled from a zoo.
The pleasure drives me mad, suffering,
sadness.
I bite with my barbarous teeth.
I am an offspring of society.
That's it! I've digested, but what does that
mean?
The roaring sea bursts forth toward me.
I struggle, trapped in the jaws of blind despair
And I threaten God, threaten with hatred.

Without Humor

The spark of humor has been extinguished
in me
I, who so wanted to burst into laughter.
In these ghost-haunted regions
I am surrounded by sad fellow sufferers.
Ah! Swollen heads, accursed and starving.
God! Have mercy on their souls.
They would go to their death
For the sake of a piece of moldy bread.
How to go on living like this
Without humor, like beasts?
There is but one remedy: Death or madness!
Yet rebellious despair still groans!

The Marysin Plain

On the Marysin plain
Covered with a cloak of snow
Mist floats, hovers silently.
How sad the fate of nature!
God has dressed the earth in winter garb.
Listen to the silence. Life is frozen.
Under the hard layer of ice
Sleeping under the heavy glass
Awaken with the coming of pleasant spring.
Your hearts, crushed under the weight of
a tyrant,
Still beat, with a faint pulse
For you still have the spirit of creation.
As tiny creatures, rise up and stand erect,
Give your fragile bodies as a gift to spring,
And your eyes, open them wide to the world.
First winds will cradle you gently,
And rain, flowing strongly, will drench you.
In the meantime, sleep, living creatures,
Until golden dawn and reviving morning
breezes
Come to awaken you from your slumber.
Prisoner of frost and ice,
The plain of Marysin dozes.
How cruel is nature's fate!
Death has cradled life in its arms,
Drained the sap of creativity.
Under the ice I hear the beating of hearts.
Life has stopped. Death has slipped

Beneath the steaming cloak.
Above the desolate plain
The silence of sorrow.
His Majesty acts in sadness...
Where life once flourished
Where green grass quivered,
Death advances within the terror,
Creativity has congealed at the height of its
fervor.
On the Marysin plain wrapped in silence,
I make my way into the distant fog.
The wild wind whirls in a satanic dance,
Its face harder than steel.
All its warmth is frozen, petrified.
The plants under the glass
Cluster together in a jumble
And the gardens seem alive.
Life has stopped, grown numb and inert,
Under the blows of the hangman.
The sun illuminates it with its soft rays
Before the dress of white covers it again.

The Ghetto Freezes

Collapsed walls will salute the conquerors
And heaps of debris will watch their
victory march.
They will discover the Pompeii of our time.
No one will blow trumpets in their honor.
Under the ruins of houses the large
Graveyard of humankind will be exposed.
In front of their terrified eyes
The frozen ghetto will appear.
They will not understand this awful spectacle
The victors of our time.
They will not be able to understand our
dreadful suffering.
Will not understand the fear, or the
darkness, or the overcrowding.
They will not feel the greedy hunger
that gnawed at us
And in their silence, they will honor the dead.
They will remain standing in front of the
frightening sight,
And then they will celebrate their
enormous triumph
And become inebriated with the joy of victory

Death

Do not embrace me, death, I want to live!
My body may be dead, but my heart beats yet.
I still want to hold on to my life
And you give off the smell of decay.
Go to rule the earth of the bereaved.
I have two eyes and hands – nightmare,
nuisance,
You do not move away from me –
holes light up in you,
You are sad, terrible, dreadful, please, go away!
Your eyes are two black spots
And the emptiness in them dwells, whines,
terrifies,
Hypnotizes and exhausts the soul.
Do not dare to glare at me.
Go, despot, to rule over your world!

I want to live, although my wings are
broken – Indeed, I have been trapped
alive in a terrible net.
I have but one more hour to take leave
of the world,
A spark of my existence still flickers inside me,
And faint life still burns within me
That always, unchanging, flows through me.

A Jew
May 12, 1944

The face is as yellow as the shameful
Star of David
The yellow patch, the Jew's mark of slavery.
The yellow clogs and the crumbling soul:
A wretched man for whom they've
sewn a patch.
The terrified eye that has no more tears
The silent heart that bleeds no more.

At what port has unshakeable faith anchored!
Hah! they march, and they live!
Masks, marked by their lives of misery
And the decay of suffering.
A living dead man, slow and deaf
A soul without a spark.
A Jew.
Accursed, inert, suspicious.
The years have struck him like a whip,
and he shakes with age.
Emaciated bones protrude from his skin.

Jevrei! Jude! Juif!
In all the lands – the same hatred.
Our frightened behavior,
Our flowing tears and laments,
Our anxieties and cat-like shrewdness,
Reflected in our tearful eyes –
All these infuriate them
And they march, and they live.

The Christian of our Time

Give me, God, the genius of the universe, flood his soul with holy passion. Mark the sign of the star on his glowing forehead, and in his mouth place the gift of the sublime word – a new savior to drift upon the poisoned earth! Wearing a halo of truth, he will not descend to the tainted ground, and like the rays of the sun, will penetrate the darkness with his words. He will be the Christian of our time. The earlier reforms have decayed, and the winds that blow in today's world he will turn into fine dust. The old, disease-ridden regimes will collapse like stacks of cards. The blind blackness and the militant madness will bow their heads before the eternal truth. The darkness will disperse, the light will burst forth, the savior, the Christian, will expose the treachery and corruption

MEMORIES

LUCIE CYTRYN-BIALER

For Sigmund
and for Nellie

August 1937. Coming Back From Vacation.

We are waiting for Grandfather and Grandmother. This year, Vienna (to be more accurate, Semmering) was the last stop on their trip. In the summer they always travel abroad, for two months. We are hanging crepe paper streamers and signs reading "Welcome home." In the kitchen, they are cleaning and preparing. The living room is full of flowers. What joy! A celebration! They're return-ing! The whole family is at the train station. The "black locomotive" that brings our loved ones closer, the "black locomotive" that will later take us to Auschwitz, Treblinka, Mydanek. How we loved to recite those lines by Tuwim[40] in school!

> The locomotive's at the platform
> Heavy and huge, it sweats
> Greasy oil.

Grandmother and Grandfather always return at the end of August, the month when we will be deported from the ghetto. Endless nightmares. The last time I parted from those I loved was at the Auschwitz train station. Joy and happiness. We wave our handkerchiefs. The "black locomotive" pulls into the station, carrying our beloved grandparents. From the car window they send us kisses. The grandchildren jump with joy. They are waiting impatiently for gifts!

A carriage harnessed to a horse waits for Grandfather and Grandmother. There are always oxygen tanks next to the driver. That's the carriage I'm so proud of, the one that will later cause me embarrassment. The principal of our

[40] Julian Tuwim (1894-1953), a Polish poet of Jewish extraction.
  Among his poems, "The Locomotive."

233

school, Miss Rein, asked me one day why I come to school in a carriage (the Yosef-Ab school in Lodz was thought to have leftist, even pre-Communist tendencies): "Madame Principal," I replied audaciously and self-confidently, "My grandfather is asthmatic, he chokes in the tram and needs a lot of air!" (I love to look at him in winter, when he wears his hat and fur coat, to be more exact, a coat lined with fur that reaches to his ankles). "And what do poor people do when they have asthma?" Miss Rein asks. "They have to take the tram," I replied, abashed. From that day on, I came to school on foot or by tram.

The managers of Cytryn Brothers, a company that processed cotton fabric, emptied it entirely early in September 1939. They came to our home and ordered us to place all of our belongings on trucks. And to think that for four years we had trusted them! The trucks were loaded with our jewelry, furs, and money. We were abducted, as simple as that. Ten kilometers from Lodz, in the forest, they told us to get off, on the pretext that we had to undergo a road check. Our managers, our erstwhile friends, abandoned us there, in the middle of nowhere, destitute. We did not even have clothing to protect us from the cold and rain. They drove away in trucks loaded with all our property, although they were supposed to have taken us to Warsaw.

Fortunately, Grandfather had remained in the apartment, because he was having a bad attack of asthma. My Aunt Rutha and my father took turns giving him oxygen. We returned from the forest. Our apartment had already been confiscated. We saw our neighbor loading packages on a truck. My mother asked him where he was going. "To Belchatow," he replied, "I have family there. You can buy bread and other things there." Without hesitating, Father put us on the truck. "Take my family to Belchatow," he said. He himself stayed in Lodz. His place was with his father, the head of the family. Mother took two rings with her. Father, his eyes filled with tears, kissed us fervently. "We'll meet again soon." Like calves who don't know why, we let the truck lead us in the middle of the night to Belchatow, to the absolute unknown.

I loved life in that town very much. All the inhabitants would meet in the market. I had many friends, I didn't go to school, I felt free. I had no homework, no piano lessons. I went everywhere alone, without a governess accompanying me. My new friends were happy, and together we organized little performances. I recited poems and Avraham wrote from morning to night. I gorged myself on cakes, especially cheesecakes. Mother, worried, waited for some word from Father. At the end of December a telegram arrived: Grandfather had passed away. My father was the only one allowed to accompany his father's body to the cemetery; at that time, Jews were already forbidden to hold funerals.

We left Belchatow. Mother knew a Polish family, who for a large sum of money agreed to take us back to Lodz in the middle of the night, in a truck again. We returned to our city in 1940, and went into the ghetto right away. Avraham never stopped writing.

We thought that in our family no one would ever have to look for an apartment. Our factories were in the area of the ghetto. One part of our family moved into 44 Wolborska Street, another part into 50 Brezezinska Street (most of the family moved to Warsaw).

On the first floor of 50 Brezezinska Street, at one time

an improvised synagogue had been set up next to Grandfather's room. Since he was asthmatic, he could not take the commotion wherever a great many people congregated. But when a window was cut out of the wall, he could hear the prayers from his bed without having to go to the synagogue. When he moved to Number forty, November 11 Street I think that was in 1936 – he was very sorry to leave behind the comfortable prayer room he had in the previous apartment. "Because of you, my children, I was forced to leave. You didn't like the neighborhood," he would say again and again.

When we got to the ghetto, we all moved into 50 Brezezinska Street. In the prayer room, the Cytryn, Rosenbloom and Pankovski families all lived together.

We did not need the services of the housing bureau. But about three months later, again we were asked to pack our belongings. The Germans were going to set up a knitwear workshop in our factory and our apartment. My father, who had not yet lost his pride – the pride of the owner's son – began shouting: Isn't this huge factory enough for the Germans. Do they need the owner's house too?! There's no point in arguing, the Jews in charge replied. We went out with our bundles. Unlike us, that part of the family that had moved to Wolbroska Street did not have to worry. There they took only the factory.

In the office where the Cytryn brothers used to hold their meetings – a beautiful office, entirely upholstered in crimson antelope leather, decorated with golden frames and equipped with a safe and mahogany furniture – lived my grandmother. The Germans confiscated only the factory, that same building my brother loved so much. We had no choice; we went to the housing bureau. There the officials had nothing to offer us. Only dingy little apartments were left. They gave us – to Mother, Father, Abraham and me – a small room, which we had to share with a lone woman. Mother nearly went out of her mind. At night that woman would rummage around in the cupboard where we kept our food. Mother slept with the sugar and bread hidden under her pillow. In 1941, there was still something to buy in the stores.

A year later, we got a room on Starosikawska Street, where some years later I would find my brother's poems. This time we didn't have anyone sharing our apartment or rummaging in our cupboard, but then we no longer had any food to keep in it…poverty was everywhere. Father died of starvation, literally, on November 11, 1942. He was 42 years old.

I have a feeling that all the poems my brother wrote about funerals were inspired by my father's death.

For the first time in my life I saw a dead body…I was afraid of my own father! I was afraid to look at him. Why? I don't have a single picture of my father, only one of my brother and mother. And I also have a picture – probably the only one in the world – that shows us getting into a cattle car at the Marysin train station (Lodz, August, 1944). In it, Mother, 44 years old, looks all bent over, and I am supporting her. Behind us stands my brother, holding on to his school bag that contained his notebooks (his greatest treasure), and on his back he's carrying a pot! I received this picture in an envelope, with an anonymous letter attached to it. I tore up the letter, but I kept the picture (it was at the end of April 1945). I suspect that one of the factory managers, who joined the German army during the war, wrote the anonymous letter.

When I returned to Lodz from the camp in eastern Prussia, I learned that my Aunt Rutha and her husband, Max Gottlieb, were still alive. A man called Bialer – my husband for forty years – gave me their address.

My aunt and uncle passed the war in Czestochova. As soon as we met, all three of us hurried to the cemetery. I showed them the graves of the members of our family who died in the ghetto. At once, my uncle ordered tombstones for each of them. Since he was penniless, he borrowed the money. All of our dead received gray tombstones.

I asked my uncle to accompany me to our apartment in the ghetto, on Starosikawska Street.

We came to the entrance of the house. Scaffolding showed that they were about to destroy or repair it. At the time, we lived on the ground floor. This time we went in through the window. People were yelling: They're crazy! It's forbidden to go inside!

My uncle collected all of Avraham's notebooks that were scattered on the floor. I was stunned with grief and remained standing near the window. In the ghetto we had also had a small plot of land. My mother used to plant potatoes there; she never shut an eye at night, for fear that someone would steal them. Now I gazed around the tiny apartment. On the floor I noticed my certificate from the Yozef-Ab high school.

My uncle took his jacket off and carefully wrapped everything he found there. We wept like children.

I went out of there like a madwoman. The next day I went to visit the building we had lived in before the war. I spoke to the concierge. It seemed as if everyone had learned the same text by heart: Ah! You're back? We were told you'd all been killed. You're at least the second one to return. But you can't go into the apartment, other people are living there now.

I froze like a statue. Suddenly I saw our neighbor, Mrs. B. Ah, you're here, so they didn't murder all of you! Not a single word of compassion, nothing. As if nothing had happened. In a shaking voice, I asked her if anyone had found any pictures. "Ah, yes, of course," Mrs. B. replied. "My daughter found one. I think it's a picture of your brother. Wait at the entrance, please." Mrs. B. was kind enough to bring me Avraham's picture. And I swore I would never set foot in that house again. I kissed the picture of my little brother, wetting it with tears. I still cherished a secret hope that he'd return. With the picture in my hand, I went towards Grandfather's apartment. We used to live across the street.

Number forty November 11 Street. Before the war, the Geir family lived in part of the first floor, and the Cytryn family in the other part. I looked at the windows, searching for my grandfather's silhouette on the balcony, where he used to sit to rest.

Now the building was guarded by a new concierge. I rang the bell. A very pleasant woman opened the door. I introduced myself and shyly asked if I could look around the apartment. The woman invited me in warmly. I crossed the rooms like a ghost, touching the walls, kissing the doors. But where are the two huge living rooms? Had the apartment shrunk? Yes, the woman replied. They've divided it into several units.

I chose to leave. In the yard I saw in my mind's eye the last family party – celebrating the engagement of my cousin Lolek and his fiancée Fela.

I lifted my eyes and saw the long balcony, where our

succah always stood all year long, decorated with crepe paper streamers. I recalled how Father would go in first, and after him, the entire family.

I remembered my grandmother. The last time I saw her was in the Litzmannstadt ghetto, in the soup line. That was in 1943. Everyone had a simple bowl, but my grandmother was holding a flat plate, and on it a soup plate, part of her dinner service that was embellished with the monogram M.Z. The last time I saw my mother and brother was at the Auschwitz railway station.

That night in the train was horrible; we arrived covered in excrement and urine, crammed together like sardines, and I was clinging to Mother. Father was lucky that he had died in his bed, Mother said again and again.

My brother kept repeating the same question: Why didn't I carry out my plan? Why? I thought he was fantasizing, but now after I've read his poems, I understand everything. When we were in the ghetto he wanted to take his own life, but he gave up on that plan because he took pity on Mother.

In one of his poems, he writes about a mother mourning her son the poet. In one of his short stories he describes a small, charming house that he particularly liked. It was in one of the lower-class neighborhoods of Lodz, behind the factory. The young people didn't want to live there. They all preferred the center of the city. The factories were in the Baluti quarter. Aaron and Tobias, my great uncle, remained faithful to the family tradition. The neighborhood wasn't important to them. Their father, Lazer-Mordechai Cytryn, lived here; it was their kingdom. In 1944, the Germans dragged them by their beards because they refused to leave the house at 44 Wolborska

Street. During the war, the factory on Wolborska Street became a carpet workshop. Carpets were manufactured from rags…that's where Grandmother was a housewife during the war. I look back and remember her. A carriage harnessed to horses waits outside; she is taking us to the Yiddish theater to see the famous play "Mirele Efrat". Always the same subject: the mean daughter-in-law who drives away her mother-in-law. Grandmother brought a whole collection of handkerchiefs with her, and cried endlessly during the play. I was bored.

In 1937, Hitler expelled the Jews of Polish extraction from Germany. He sent them, carrying only small bundles of their belongings, to the Polish border, to the city of Zvonshin. There, they spent two nights. At the time, life in Poland was still peaceful. The young Jews who arrived from Germany still of school age were dispersed among the Jewish schools. Our two principals, Misses Rubinstein and Rein, informed us that the pupils who came from Germany would be joining our classes. They suggested that at first we speak German to them, until they become used to our language, to the new rules, and to our sorrow – to our hard lives too. Our principals also asked us to show solidarity and to invite them to meals in our homes. The poor little girls who came from Germany!

I remember that I invited a German friend, the daughter of a well-known industrialist, to dinner at our home. She came, looking wretched. During the meal, my father asked many questions. Mother had tears in her eyes. But that didn't keep us from eating a fine meal, sighing from time to time, and caressing little Gerda.

The only one who ate nothing was my brother Avraham. He left the dining room, slamming the door, and shut himself up in his room.

1945. I looked at my aunt, who was pregnant, her belly swelling. I hadn't read my brother's poems. The war had just ended. Perhaps he'll still return?

On the day of my engagement, all the guests came, but I forgot them. I had gone to the cinema with a friend to see "Gone with the Wind." I liked the movie so much that we stayed for the second show. My fiancé took the disappointment with humor, my aunt was furious, and I ate a piece of cake with pleasure.

I remember the first time I went to the market with Rutha. I heard someone say that you have to blow on a chicken to see if it's fat. I was as afraid of those chickens as I was of fire. I began to blow on the chicken's head. A peasant woman who saw me yelled: "Are you stupid? You have to blow on its backside." I bought one, tied a rope to its leg and walked with it as if it were a puppy. Everyone looked at me, and I suddenly heard my aunt screeching: "A catastrophe! Your fiancé is standing across the street. What a drama!" I just went on walking, and Mr. Bialer waved hello to me from afar, as if nothing had happened. I returned his greeting and went home with my chicken.

On October 14, 1945, our wedding was celebrated. Sigmund Bialer and Lucie Cytryn. My aunt organized the ceremony in her apartment. I cried. I didn't want that wedding! Without Mother, without Father, without Avraham, without family! My wedding dress was dark blue. Rutha did her best so that I'd at least wear a white collar and white lace.

1945-1946. After a visit to Dr. Libo in Lodz, Sigmund decided my tonsils had to be removed. He spoke to me as if I were a child: Don't be afraid, it will sting a bit and that's all. I went to the clinic as if I were going to the slaughter house. The operation did hurt. When I looked at Dr. Libo, I began to cry. I had the feeling I was back before the war, and was looking again at the face of Dr. Bronikowski, the doctor Mother took me to in 1938, who then recommended my tonsils be removed. Dr. Libo couldn't understand why I was reacting that way.

My husband was certain that I was crying because of the operation. He embraced me, wiped away my tears and said, laughing: "Stop crying like a little girl! I wonder why your mother didn't take care of your tonsils." If he could have seen the pictures that were moving past my eyes!

Auschwitz. We were covered with excrement and urine. There were screams. Mothers searching for their children. The locomotive stopped. Mother kept pushing sugar into Avraham's mouth.

Throughout the whole period of our stay in the ghetto, Mother always hid small portions of sugar. When the Germans began to yell: Left! Right! The women on one side, the children on the other side, the men to move forward, I saw how Mother was pushing sugar into Avraham's mouth.

That was the last time I saw him. In one hand he was clutching the bag containing his poems. Mother and I were in the same "selection." She never stopped saying: How fortunate that Father died in his bed. I held on to her arm, but there was an S.S. officer in front of us, a satanic smile on his face: "*Mutter und Tochter, gerade muss ich trennen*" (I'm the one who has to separate between mother and daughter). I hugged Mother as hard as I could. It's my fault! Until today I still blame myself. She looked at me,

"My sweet one, put the scarf around your neck, you're coughing."

When my daughter was six, I told her this story. This dramatic scene has haunted me throughout my life.

The "black locomotive". The old people didn't feel well. *"Rechts, links"* (Right, Left). Heartrending screams of mothers separated from their beloved children. Bestial screams! Women lay on the ground holding on to their children. They were shot on the spot. I looked to the left. The small children cried out in a chorus, spontaneously. Some were carrying a doll or some other favoriet toy, some were smiling. A barbaric female S.S. officer marched at the head of the line. Maybe it's just an outing? The children thought. "Mother! Father" they cried out. I wept, not understanding where I was.

In the ghetto, when my little brother and I stood at the window, Catholic children would tease us from across the barbed wire fences. They would take big bites out of slices of bread spread with lard and sing:

With an ax, a saw, with pruning shears
Today we'll chop off the Jews' ears.

Now I turned around and around trying to find my mother's gaze. I didn't know I wasn't allowed to move out of the line. An S.S. woman hit me on the head. I must have lost consciousness. I don't remember seeing the sign that read *"Arbeit macht frei."*[41] I only remember that they bent our heads over a barrel and cut our hair off with large machines, as if we were sheep. We were naked. Around my neck, I had a gold chain with a small heart that had my name engraved on it. Luisa. My grandfather had bought a chain like that for each of his granddaughters. He'd

[41] Work Brings Freedom

ordered them made with a special clasp so that they could never be removed. The German woman became enraged when she couldn't remove the chain and began pulling it until she wounded me. I thought she was going to choke me. Then one of her friends came, a terrifying woman accompanied by someone who may have been a man or a woman; I couldn't tell. Finally they cut the chain off. I had blood on my neck, but I didn't have a bandage. I was so terrified, my bowels loosened.

Before the war, Avraham, unlike me, did not eat anything. You had to literally cram food down his mouth. Father would pat his head and say: "Eat, eat, so you'll be strong. You need to grow and be a strong man, because you'll be my heir." One day my parents wanted to force him to eat soup with dumplings. He stood on the chair, screamed and cried out: "Murderers! Mother is really a medusa, and Father is behaving like Hitler! Stop torment-ing me. The crybaby will eat everything in a minute, give her my soup, she's been eyeing my plate like a witch."

My brother always criticized me, and we fought all the time. One day, when Mother came home, she found a real duel going on. She was angry. "What do mothers with lots of children do?" she yelled. My brother, who was sunk deep into a large armchair, dangling his little feet, gave my mother a mischievous look and said quietly, "And what do mothers do when they have lots of children and no ser-vants?" "Listen, crybaby," my brother suggested to me one day, "I really can't stand this silk shirt with the stiff collar and that hairdo with bangs. I'm going to compose a little poem to the governess, and while she's reading it, you'll cut my hair. In return, I'll help you open the sideboard with a knife, I know where the chocolate is hidden."

The sweets were locked up so that I wouldn't gorge myself on them. His suggestion frightened me, and I tried to talk him out of it. "You remember how Mother yelled at the governess for taking a photo of you in your beach sandals? You've dressed the boy like a clown," she said.

"Yes," he replied, "but I can't stand this stiff collar and these velvet pants! I'm sick of looking like a rich kid! I'm begging you, crybaby, cut my hair and you'll get a lot of chocolate…" Since I was a real glutton, I agreed.

We began carrying out our plan. I sat at the piano. Mother went out, very happy to see I was practicing, and that my brother was asking for his four o'clock snack (he, who never agreed to eat anything). Here, she was winning! Lucie at the piano and Avraham at the table! The world was hers. As soon as the door closed behind her, Avraham handed the poem to Zoshia, our governess. "I wrote this for you," he said politely. "Please, go into your room, because I'm preparing another surprise." In the meantime, I continued cheerfully banging at the piano. When Zoshia disappeared, we took the knife, and wack! opened the splendid walnut sideboard. With a mouth full of cookies and pockets crammed full of chocolate, I took the scissors from Avraham's hands. "Cut, crybaby, quickly, so I'll finally look like a normal boy!"

I energetically undertook the task. I had barely started when I stabbed his ear. He screamed. Zoshia came running. "What are you two doing in the bathroom? Open the door at once." By this time, my brother only had half his bangs, and the other half had lost its shape. Everyone was yelling, and I was contentedly eating my chocolate. When the servants noticed the broken sideboard, bedlam broke loose in the house. What should we do? When did they do this? What will Madam say? Zoshia shouted. This boy looks like a plucked chicken!

In the evening, Mother returned home. I was crying with fright. Avraham, on the other hand, was sitting calmly, not the least bit worried. Mother felt ill.

But, in contrast, at the Auschwitz railway station she didn't lose her composure for a minute. "Children, don't forget you have underwear to change into." She also remained calm when Father was dying of hunger and fatigue, on November 11, 1942. She asked us not to cry. "There's a war going on, you're young, you'll go to school," she said. She forced us to do our homework. "It will help you in life, children." Our principal, Miss Rein, founded a school in the Lodz ghetto. I was preparing for matriculation examinations…

In my imagination, I will always hear myself saying to Mother: "Mother, please stop these lessons, I'm dying of hunger." Mother would glance around the room, tear a piece of plaster off the wall and say: "Imagine this is a piece of sugar."

After Father died, Avraham became conscious of his role as the head of the family. Thanks to him, Mother found work in one of the public kitchens, where she peeled potatoes (a job everyone dreamed of). "I don't understand you," Avraham said one day to Mother, banging his fist on the table. "Everyone is jealous of me because my mother has been working in a kitchen for two months, and you, you haven't even stolen one potato." "That's true, but I give you my bread ration, because I eat soup twice a day," Mother replied. "All right, but starting tomorrow, I want you to measure the bread in centimeters. You always give Lucie more!" "No, my son, I always divide it into equal parts, but if you want, I'll measure the bread in centimeters to be sure both pieces are the same."

The following day, Mother returned from work as pale as chalk. She was close to fainting. From her sleeve, she slid out two potatoes the size of a nut. When Avraham saw them, he kissed her hands. "Don't do it anymore, Mother. I don't want you to get sick. You'll see, the Russians or someone else will liberate us. Don't cry, little mother, our Pik-Cytryn princess. You'll see, everything will be all right, the world won't let us die. Dearest mother, don't cry!"

An hour later, hunger began to torment Avraham again. He was fifteen, at the peak of his growth. He looked at me with malicious eyes. He had a piercing look: "And you? Everyone tells me I have a beautiful sister. What good does that do me? Why don't you become the mistress of one of the privileged ones in the ghetto?" I replied that Mother always told me that to go out with a man, you have to love him. "That's true my daughter, that's really what I taught you. But now there's a war, a terrible war. Try to understand Avraham, he's growing, he's hungry. If Father had had what to eat, he wouldn't have died. What a nightmare!"

I was stunned. You raised me like a nun, and now you want me to…I thought to myself. I fell asleep like a log. The next day I cursed and cursed when Mother came to wake me to go to work. I was in the middle of a dream, eating potato and beet soup. I ate so much in the dream, I was nearly full.

At the center of the ghetto, there was a house called the little red house. That was the location of the *Kriminalpolizei*, the criminal police. They'd bring people there to torture them. One morning, they came to take

Mother. They took her from the house despite our tears. We remained alone in our miserable, gloomy room. Suddenly I recalled that a friend of mine lived opposite the red house, on the third floor. I remembered the family name: Adler. I stood behind the curtain at her home, and managed to see Mother. She had a hard time walking. I sobbed. But it wasn't ordinary sobbing, more like the bleating of a lamb about to be slaughtered. The next day I couldn't see Mother anymore from my observation post.

Four days went by without Mother. In the ghetto, Avraham stopped calling me crybaby. "Sit down, Lucie," he said to me, "I have something to say to you. I know a man who has connections. You've got to go talk to him. Give him whatever he wants, do you understand?" "Are you sure about what you're saying, Avraham? The man you're sending me to is old, fat and disgusting!" "Go anyway. They may be torturing Mother at this very moment…Go and see what you can do." I went.

I knocked shyly at the door. My heart was beating so hard I thought it would burst. The door opened, and standing in front of me was not a man, but a bear. I began to stutter and shake. I told him my story. He asked me dryly when they had taken Mother. "Five days ago, sir." He pinched my cheek. "You're awfully pretty," he said in Polish with a repulsive Yiddish accent. Redfaced and perspiring, he looked intensely in my eyes, breathing like a beast and smelling of sweat. "Listen, little one, your mother will be home tomorrow, at the latest the day after." I stood in front of him, as motionless as a marble statue.

He threw me on to the bed. I was dying of fear. He hurt me terribly. The man was as wild as a lion. I gritted my teeth and clenched my fists. I cried when I thought of

Mother returning the next day. He crushed me with his heavy body. I yelled with pain.

I ran home quickly, eager to tell Avraham that I had done everything he told me to. I was literally torn to bits. Everything hurt me, I was nauseous, I was starving, but happy. I opened the door. Mother was there. I kissed her. It was hard for her to talk. She was lying on her bed, as white as chalk. I kissed her hands and face. She had been released three hours earlier. My sacrifice had been in vain. Avraham was at work. Why had he sent me to that filth? And why had I gone? Mother suddenly turned over in bed, and the blanket slid off her. Her buttocks were as black as coal. I stopped thinking about what had happened. God, how much she had suffered. Our queen! I cried hot tears. "My dear mother," I said to her, and knelt over her. "They wanted to know where I had hidden the Cytryn jewels," she said in a feeble voice.

Avraham returned from work. He looked at me without saying a word, but he understood. I told him everything. "It's not so bad," he said. "I'm sorry I sent you there, but I had no way of knowing when Mother would be released." "Please, Avraham, let's not talk about it anymore." That wound, which has remained a secret until today, left its imprint on me for the whole of my life.

September 1939. I was standing in line for bread when a German roughly assaulted us: "*Juden*! Get out of the line!" I didn't move, but our neighbor pointed to me. She had known me since I was born. She pointed to me three times. I was dragged out by my hair and taken to wash floors in our school. It was the first time in my life that I had done that kind of work. I was in the recess room of the school. How could this be? I looked all around naively.

Maybe the principal would come in. Maybe she'd come to save me. But there was no longer anyone in the school. The minute I raised my head, I was beaten with a whip.

There, in our high school, where model pupils, happy pupils showed respect for their teachers by curtsying...I looked to the right again. Maybe the janitor Andrej was still there? I went down to scrub the floor in the gym. In my imagination I saw, as if I were really touching them, the white blouses and blue gym bloomers of the pupils. And the teacher, Segal, with her whistle. Maybe one of the teachers – Mr. Streisberger, Mr. Biran, Mr. Levy, Mr. Koriansky – would come in? I wished one of them would come in, only not the mathematics teacher, Mr. Nahuma! Ah! I was really frightened of mathematics. The course I liked best was the religion lessons given us by Mr. Goldberg. I never listened to anything. We would tell our love stories, read to one another our first romantic letters.

The whip lashed at my head. "*Schneller!*"[42]

It was not a good idea to raise my head. We scrubbed the floor crouching on our knees. I was young, nothing hurt me, but an old man, a bearded Jew, worked next to me, breathing hard. A soldier grabbed him by his beard. "*Schneller!*"

1947. When I returned from vacation, the doctors told me I was pregnant, in my second month. Pregnant! A new drama: Don't read your brother's poems, you mustn't be sad. The baby needs calm! I strolled about the streets of Lodz, crying. I'm pregnant, and my parents won't see the baby. What's the point of bringing a child into the world if they'll kill it? I said to myself.

[42] Faster!

251

I sat next to my husband in a warm café. I cried. I told him about a horrible scene from the camp: A young woman gave birth to a child there. The birth took place in the open air. A German woman showed the newborn infant to the mother, and then brutally wrapped it in a diaper, choking it to death. I can't forget the mother's tears, I see her all the time and hear her cries: *"Mein kind! Mein kind!"*

We lived in Lodz until 1950. My husband managed the family lumber business. He very much wanted to join his sisters in Paris, where they had gone before the war to study, and to live near them. One of his brothers, Pinek, had survived Auschwitz. He too was living in Paris.

Unfortunately, our papers had been confiscated. We could only leave Poland by immigrating to Israel, via Gdynia. We sailed to Haifa. I was in the spa city of Krinitza, together with my daughter, when my husband informed me – it was at the end of August – that we had a place on the ship. We could only take a small amount of luggage. We had to leave behind nearly all the contents of our apartment. Again and again I heard the refrain: "The Jewboys are on the roads again." When my husband saw me packing salami, he got angry: "If we're going to a country where poverty awaits us, we'd better commit suicide right now! There'll be everything there. I don't want you to take any food."

At the railway station, a customs official wanted to confiscate my brother's poems. I began to shout so loudly that they could probably hear me all the way to Haifa. "Aren't you ashamed," I yelled, "Do you want to take my family away from me?" I spilled all of my anger at him. "Read all these little pages. It's my brother's diary, that's all. He wrote

252

in Polish. It's all that's left of my family. And I won't give it to you even if you bring the army here!" Nellie tugged at the official's jacket, "I've got a stomachache," she said. In the end, he let us go without confiscating anything. My cousins, Yanke and Chenyo, gave the little one a hand while I gathered up all of Avraham's notebooks.

The black locomotive took us to Gdynia. Exhausted from the journey, we boarded the ship, after a three-hour wait. "My whole life has been one big rush," my husband said: "Within 24 hours I must leave Poland, within two days I must be at this or that place, within ten days I must submit this or that document..."

Late in September 1950 we drew near to Haifa. Our hearts pounded. Our country! The land of Israel! Suddenly I heard a voice that clearly came from the direction of the sea. "Bialer! Bialer!" My husband who was convinced that the journey had jeopardized my sanity, tried to calm me. But suddenly people turned towards us: "Someone is calling a person called Bialer. Do you hear?" The echo grew stronger, and the voice became clearer. This time I thought my husband had gone mad. "Perhaps someone wants us to return to Poland? Perhaps some special committee is summoning me?" he called out. "I don't believe it, you're losing your mind. What are you talking about? We've been outside the territorial waters of Poland for days!"

Suddenly all the people on the deck began to wave their handkerchiefs. A boat was approaching. For the first time in my life I saw an Israeli soldier, standing erect and saluting. "Welcome, shalom! I'm looking for my uncle, Bialer!" My husband bent over the ship's railing. I held my daughter in my arms. "Who are you?" "I'm Ilan, Uncle Sigmund, the son of your brother Shimon. I remained alive after Auschwitz." He climbed up a ladder, boarded the ship and threw himself into my husband's arms. "Uncle Sigmund, I wanted to surprise you." He was thirteen when they took him to Auschwitz. All the people on the ship cried. Afterwards we all sang HaTikvah. I knew we wouldn't stay in Israel. Sigmund wanted to be close to his family in Paris. There was food rationing then in Israel. It was what they called the austerity period. People made vegetable soup as if they were building a house – with the help of materials from the threshing floor and from the vineyard – potatoes from Jaffa, carrots from Petach Tikvah…one day at five in the morning, I heard the neighbors shouting in a mixture of Polish and Hebrew: Carps have arrived, people are standing in line! I had the impression that we were at war again and had gone back to the system of food rationing.

I also remember that once I miraculously managed to obtain American noodles in the shape of the letters of the alphabet. Nellie had just come back from a walk. With her alert gaze, she looked at the soup and noticed the little letters floating in it. "What, do you want me to eat a newspaper?" And in a fell swoop, she turned over her plate and poured its contents on the floor. "I'm not eating books or newspapers! Give me soup!"

August 29, 1944. Auschwitz. Monkeys with shaven heads, a number tattooed on their arms, stand in the sun after the journey in cattle cars. They handed out herrings. The sun was mercilessly beating down on us. We were divided into groups of five. We were thirsty. Frightened. Where were our families? Where were we?

They gave the monkeys, all of us, one small cup of water. Each one pulled it towards her. The water spilled on the floor. The first pushes, the first reflexes of survival. Each one wanted to wet her lips. Each one pounced on the cup. The first animal-like instinct.

Young German S.S. women rolled with laughter, as if they were at the circus. Half human beings, half beasts. Bravo! The thrust of a razor over our heads, and the girls become animals.

In the ghetto at least we had a room or an apartment. We suffered, but we were still human. We said thank you, we said pardon me, we washed, we changed our underwear...but here, in Auschwitz, we became real monsters.

In front of me I saw my two cousins in prisoners' clothing. They supported one another. I recalled the last family party we had. By mistake, the seamstress had made them identical dresses. When they entered the living room, they nearly fainted. What a scandal! They were ready to kill the seamstress. They were consoled by the promise that they'd be put in separate rooms. There was weeping and fainting. And now in Auschwitz, they wear the same uniform and beg to stay together!

I will never forget the look on my brother's face when we parted: Lucie, take good care of Mother! He had tears in his eyes, and his nostrils quivered. In a second he was gone. I clung to mother, and that was my biggest mistake. *Gerade Tochter und Mutter* – they must be separated. I stayed in Auschwitz several days, maybe two weeks. I can't remember exactly. We were both in shock. It turned out that our transport was one of the last. They didn't tattoo a number on our arms. I searched for Mother the whole time. We had no idea where we were, nor did we know what to expect. Hungarian and Czech Jewish women, who had been there for two years, told us we had come to a family pension…we slept in barracks, while they, when they had arrived at the camp, slept on packed snow. These women were exhausted, they had deteriorated to the level of animals.

One morning, I think it was in November, they handed out dresses. Long dresses for short women, short dresses for tall women. We were barefoot, we had no underwear. We dripped from everywhere. We were transferred to Stutthof. I will never forget that journey.

They threw us into cattle cars that had been used to transport coal. They were full of dust and still horribly warm. They gave us margarine, just stuck a lump of it into our hands. We traveled for 24 hours, maybe even more. For us, time no longer existed. We were exhausted, we slept and breathed in the coal dust. The margarine melted in our hands.

When an S.S. soldier opened the lead bolts that locked our car, he burst out laughing. We were black, our heads were shaved, to him we looked like wild animals. He called to his friends, who kept pointing to us and laughing uproariously.

I am sure that if any of the survivors of our group were to read these lines, she would remember the revolting salty taste of the margarine! Our lips burned, our eyes were full of tears. We learned we were at Stutthof. I lay in bed with horrific pains. I had an abscessed sore on my hip that burned, causing me intolerable pain. I screamed like a dog. They took me to a barracks that bore the name "hospital" even though there was not a single medicine in it. On the spot, the German doctor declared that my leg had to be amputated. "*Scheisse!*" (shit) is what he said. I remember that a woman doctor – I think she was a Czech Jew – whispered in my ear: "Run away as fast as you can from this barracks, otherwise they'll cut off your leg and then get rid of you." We didn't know yet about the crematoria.

The next morning I returned to my group of "coal-black" girls. The Germans gave us no water to wash with. We were their entertainment. Those black monkeys are really very funny! From Stutthof we were transferred to Schiffenbeil in Eastern Prussia, a camp with huge buildings. The director there was a Wehrmacht, not an S.S. officer, and he treated us like human beings. That was very unusual, one out of ten million. He assigned me to work in the kitchens and the living quarters. A dream! He gave me the keys to the kitchen. I thought I would go out of my mind with joy! Now at last I'll be able to eat my fill! Suddenly I saw my cousin lying on the floor. She was fourteen but looked like eighteen.

Bronka Pik was the daughter of my uncle on my mother's side. I looked after her as if she were my sister. But fate intervened. A month later, the director of the camp told me he was leaving the next day, and would be replaced by an S.S. Oberstrumfuhrer and two S.S. women. They were two very nasty women, both of them in love with the officer, both trying to please him. The one who succeeded in accumulating more dead bodies on her shift could get to sleep with him.

One day one of these women came into the kitchen and ordered us to put into the soup the amount of margarine that was intended for a whole month. What a massacre that was! Everyone suffered from dysentery and a hundred women died in one night!

January was bitterly cold. We marched in the snow, our

feet wrapped in newspapers. On the way, the Germans shot anyone who stopped. I asked Bronka to walk next to me. No, she replied, I don't want to walk with the old women. I was twenty years old then! Running, she joined the group of girls. All of my efforts to persuade her were in vain. I suddenly heard shots from the direction she had run in. It was forbidden to look. Bronka fell together with the group of girls. The Germans shattered the layer of ice with hand grenades and threw the girls into the freezing water. One day, the black angels issued an order: to replace the boards we sat on in the toilets. We were only allowed to go into the toilets – a wretched, abominable hut – in the morning. The rest of the day we relieved ourselves straight on to the ground under us. The wooden boards were replaced, but it turned out there was a deliberate plan behind the order. Today no one knows exactly what happened, no one has heard of it, and even worse – no one is prepared to believe! The six round openings that had served us previously were replaced by three huge holes. The black angels' hope was not disappointed: many of the women fainted and fell straight into the pits of excrement. Once I was forced to go to work outside the camp. It was on the day when the two women and the Oberstrumfuhrer arrived. That day all the prisoners were ordered to get up earlier. Soldiers escorted us to a place several kilometers away from the camp. A procession of exhausted skeletons, dressed in rags and swarming with lice.

When we arrived at the work site, we found a huge pile of sand and cement. On the first day, we were ordered to move that mountain to the left, and the next day we were ordered to move it to the right. A truly Sisyphean task! It was in the midst of winter. We moved the cement, digging in the ground with shovels. In the evening we returned to the camp on foot. The black angels counted their lambs, to make sure no one had run away.

One day they noticed that two women were missing. The woman in charge of the toilets grew pale, and her whole body shook. "Two women have fallen into the toilets", she finally said. I'll never forget the satanic smile on the lips of Annie-Lote Schmidt and Trude. And then we fled. A forty-eight year old woman marched with us – to us she was old – and alongside her, her two daughters. We didn't know then what a mother is capable of doing for her children. Mrs. Spiegel thought of her daughters before anything else. When night fell, she noticed a barn. She covered us with hay, with one hand holding on to her daughters, and with the other tenderly caressing us. The next morning we had to leave there. We had no idea where we were. It had snowed all night. We were starving, frightened, frozen, in the middle of the forest. Suddenly a military vehicle drew up and an S.S. officer got out. He looked at us and drew his weapon to shoot us.

We kept quiet. We were already sick of life anyway. We didn't care if he killed us because we didn't have the strength to   struggle anymore. But when Mrs. Spiegel saw the officer getting ready to fire, she threw herself at his feet and began to shout in Russian. She tried to tell him that the Russians were going to arrive soon. Then she switched to German: When the war is over, we'll defend you! In the midst of her attack of frenzy, she suddenly began to sing in Russian. The officer who had remained in the vehicle shouted to his comrade: "Leave that shit alone already!" And the officer standing in front of us put his revolver back in its holster and returned to the car.

Afterwards we were sent to a stalag, together with prisoners of war. When I lay on my bunk, I recalled a poem my brother had once written: "Jew, *Juden, Ivrei!*[43] All of their blood has been spilled, and yet it is not enough!" Then I still believed I would see them all again. I believed with all my heart.

February 10, 1945. For us it was the end of the war.

When we left the stalag, we met Russian soldiers. We proudly informed them, in their language, that we were Jewish women. Unfortunately, the poor state of our health and our shaven heads did not impress them. They wanted only to rape us, and that's what they did. The soldiers back from the front were like wild beasts, and their passion was uncontainable.

We marched through the streets of Olstein like sleepwalkers. We met the first of the Polish officers, who looked like weird creatures, dressed in rags. We told them we had been saved by a miracle. We cried. Suddenly one of the soldiers came over to us and said to me quietly: "Stop, I'm begging you!" Then he added in a whisper, "I'm Jewish, but my comrades don't know that. Are you from Lodz? I am too. I was one of the first soldiers to liberate the city. I met a Jew there, who was my boss before the war. His name is Sigmund Bialer, and he lives on Narutowcza Street.

When Nellie was small, she always asked why there were no grandmothers and grandfathers around. I remember that in London, Nellie was invited to the home of a traditional Jewish family. Before the Friday evening meal, they all prayed. My daughter did not know a single hymn or prayer, but she was very moved and thought about my

[43] "Jew" in German and Russian.

childhood. And then the head of the family, the grandmother, who was sitting in her late husband's chair, said to her: "I see that the young Miss Bialer does not know any prayers." Nellie answered at once, in a loud voice: "I also don't know the tenderness of a grandmother." The woman, very embarrassed, got up and sat down next to my daughter. For twenty years until that evening, she had always sat in her husband's seat, and no one had ever seen her, at least not on the Sabbath, sit anywhere else. Now she caressed Nellie's head, and asked that her plate be put next to my daughter's.

Israel, 1986. A senior physician diagnosed a malignant growth in Nellie's brain. No one told us. Nellie swore that if anyone told her parents, she would take her own life. "I'm an adult," she said, "I know what's happening to me. I'll fight it and I'll get well."

Her friend, Irene Kraut and my cousin Fela telephoned the attorney, Mr. Lombard. They also made a phone call to New York. Harry, Nellie's friend, came from the United States. In mid-August, Lombard brought Professor Grizoli to Israel.

Mr. Lombard pleaded with Nellie: I want to let your parents know. "Coward!" Nellie cried. "There are moments in life when children have to protect their parents. My father was in Treblinka; my mother in Auschwitz. Let them rest peacefully in the mountains!"

Since she was a small child, Nellie had always done what she wanted, down to the last detail.

Marseilles, August 20, 1986. Nellie underwent surgery. Mr. Lombard hired the best specialists. We still knew nothing. Two days before the operation, Lombard still pleaded with her: "I'm going to visit your parents. I'll prepare them personally. We'll fly there together. I don't want to take the decision on my own. Your family (the survivors of the Cytryn and Pik families) keep telephoning me."

Nellie was furious: "Don't aggravate me before this serious operation. I don't want to kill my mother. I don't want my parents to know. You are all cowards!"

Years earlier, Nellie had hidden the things my brother had written. Nellie, who was the embodiment of strength and vitality, suffered like a martyr. My wonderful Nellie grew so thin, she looked like a twelve year old. I sat next to her all day and smiled. The first treatment was over. That nightmare had ended. I went with Nellie to her office. In the elevator, she said to me: "Mother, I love my office and my work. But the attorney Nellie Bialer is finished, it's all over." She gazed at her reflection in the mirror of the elevator. "Look how thin I am. I have only one eye." Auschwitz! Maydanek! Treblinka! I thought I was going to faint when I suddenly discovered a clump of hair on her suit. The chemotherapy had had its effect. I was agitated, but I kept smiling. "Madam attorney," and that was the first time I had addressed her like that, "Let's go home. The nurse is coming to give you an injection."

Mr. Lombard's driver was holding a folder in his hand. I noticed that it held my brother's notebooks. Nellie had brought them home. I pretended I hadn't noticed anything. We returned home. Nellie asked the driver to put the papers in a drawer, and then she locked it. An evil omen. Nellie knew she'd never be responsible for those notebooks again.

When it was all over, I was left without my Nellie. My life was over, I only had my existence. For the Jews, the mourning period lasts seven days, but I remained in a state of shock for a whole month. From morning to evening, I was surrounded by friends, some close and some less so. They read us moving telegrams: the hall of justice is in mourning, our sun has sunk, Nellie has left us. In all the letters one fact, worded in diverse ways, was repeated: Nellie loved her parents so much. We all know you from Nellie's stories, and there will never be another like her.

During her illness, her clients told me - people I didn't know and who so admired her abilities - how she had defended them. One young man brought a flower: "I never had a chance to pay Attorney Bialer," he said. "She said she'd bill me when she got better. She saved me from the clutches of drugs and crime," and he burst into tears. Personal letters, beautiful bouquets, thank-you notes. I sat silently in the room looking around me. I was surrounded by my friends, their eyes swollen from crying, all looking at pictures of Nellie. Since then we live without Nellie, for Nellie's sake.

1993. I was watching television when they showed a re-run of the testimonies given at the trial of Klaus Barbie. My husband and I looked for Nellie. Suddenly we saw her alongside Attorney Lombard. Eight months had passed since her surgery. My husband wept, I kissed the screen. In my mind's eye, I saw her as if she were still alive, standing at the door, holding her robe in her hand, ready to leave for the trial in Lyon. "Mother, I love my work, but I think this is the last time I'll wear this robe. When I see Barbie, I'll hit him." I trembled. I knew her. I knew she was capable of doing that! All of that was in 1987. Now I could only look at the tape to see my daughter listening to the witnesses. She was a lawyer, her parents had been in the death camps. If only she could speak, she would say: Why?

Jennie Nellie Bialer, 1948-1988

Nellie was born on June 4, 1948 in Lodz, Poland to Sigmund Bialer, a survivor of Treblinka, and Lucie Cytryn Bialer, a survivor of Auschwitz.

Nellie completed her secondary school studies in Paris with distinction, in the Victor Hugo school, received her bachelor's degree in law and her master's degree in privacy law, as well as a degree in business English, and she spoke six languages fluently.

Nellie, whose childhood and years of study were imbued with the atmosphere of the Holocaust, specialized in large trials dealing with war crimes. As a lawyer she was registered on the committee of the bar association in the Paris court, and began her clerkship with the attorney, Mr. Florio. Afterwards, she assisted the attorney, Mr. Lombard in large trials of war criminals.

Over time, Nellie's parents, survivors of the Holocaust, shared their secrets with her, and told her everything that had happened to them. Her mother entrusted her with Avraham Cytryn's writings for the purpose of publishing them some time in the future, but Nellie put off this task because she did not want to revive their painful memories and wished to prevent her parents from re-living their past suffering.

Nellie took it upon herself to bear this heavy burden in silence and lived with a memory of the past that was not her own. In this spirit of a child of the Holocaust, Nellie served on the prosecution team in Barbie's trial alongside Attorney Lombard.

In 1986, the doctors discovered that Nellie had a

malignant brain tumor, but she concealed her illness from her parents to save them from any further pain, feeling they had already suffered enough. Nearly totally blind, she helped Mr. Lombard complete the Barbie trial, and died on March 21, 1988, eight months after she had brain surgery.

Nellie Bialer's bitter fate clearly demonstrates the effects of the Holocaust on the second generation of survivors. Nellie's photograph in her lawyer's robes, a photograph of her mother, Lucie Cytryn-Bialer, as well as a summary of Barbie's trial were personally given to the museum in Los Angeles on the day of its opening by Mrs. Lucie Bialer.